EAST ANGLIAN ARCHAEOLOGY

Excavation of a Romano-British Settlement on the A149 Snettisham Bypass, 1989

by Myk Flitcroft

with specialist contributions from
S. Anderson, T. Ashwin, S. Cottam,
J.A. Davies, B. Dickinson,
Tony Gregory, David Gurney,
J. Hillam, D. Mackreth, G. McDonnell,
C. Mortimer, P. Murphy, J. Price and
D. Williams

and illustrations by
Steven Ashley, Dave Fox and Piers Wallace

East Anglian Archaeology
Report No.93, 2001

Archaeology and Environment Division
Norfolk Museums and Archaeology Service

EAST ANGLIAN ARCHAEOLOGY
REPORT NO.93

Published by
Archaeology and Environment Division
Norfolk Museums and Archaeology Service
Union House
Gressenhall
Dereham
Norfolk NR20 4DR

in conjunction with
The Scole Archaeological Committee

Editor: Peter Wade-Martins
Managing Editor: Jenny Glazebrook

Scole Editorial Sub-committee:
Brian Ayers, Archaeology and Environment Officer, Norfolk Museums and Archaeology Service
David Buckley, County Archaeologist, Essex Planning Department
Keith Wade, Archaeological Service Manager, Suffolk County Council
Peter Wade-Martins
Stanley West

Set in Times Roman by Joan Daniells and Jenny Glazebrook using Corel Ventura™
Printed by Witley Press Ltd., Hunstanton, Norfolk

ISBN 0 905594 31 2

For details of *East Anglian Archaeology*, see last page

This volume is published with the aid of a grant from English Heritage

Cover photograph:
Aerial view of the excavation in progress, 10 October 1989
Photo by D.A. Edwards (ref: TF6733/W)

Contents

List of Plates

List of Figures

List of Tables

List of Contributors

Sue Anderson, BA, MPhil, MIFA
Human Bone Specialist

Trevor Ashwin, BA
Senior Project Manager, Norfolk Archaeological Unit

Sally Cottam
formerly Department of Archaeology, University of Durham

John A. Davies, BA, PhD
Keeper of Archaeology, Norwich Castle Museum

Brenda Dickinson
Freelance Consultant

Myk Flitcroft, BA, MSc, MIFA
formerly Senior Project Manager, Norfolk Archaeological Unit

The late Tony Gregory, MA, AMA, MIFA

David Gurney, BA, MIFA
Principal Landscape Archaeologist, Norfolk Landscape Archaeology

Jennifer Hillam, BSc, FSA, MIFA
Dendrochronology Laboratory, Department of Archaeology and Prehistory, University of Sheffield

Gerry McDonnell, BTech, PhD
Department of Archaeological Sciences, University of Bradford

D.F. Mackreth, BA, FSA
Freelance Consultant

C. Mortimer, BTech, DPhil
Freelance Consultant

Peter Murphy, BSc, MPhil
Centre of East Anglian Studies, University of East Anglia

Jennifer Price, PhD, FSA
Department of Archaeology, University of Durham

D.F. Williams, PhD, FSA
English Heritage Ceramic and Lithic Petrology Project, Department of Archaeology, University of Southampton

Acknowledgements

The greatest debt is to the excavation and post-excavation team: Jonathan Erskine (Site Supervisor), Phil Copleston (Finds Supervisor), Melanie Gauden, Dave Hodgekinson, Mike Hurn, Michael Ings, Jamie Patrick, Jens Samuels, Simon Savage, and Lisa Wastling (Excavators); Steven Ashley, Dave Fox, and Piers Wallace (Illustrators); and all the specialist contributors to this report.

The fieldwork stage of the excavation was funded by Norfolk County Council, while the post-excavation funds were provided by English Heritage: thanks are due to Philip Walker (EH) for his championing of the analysis programme and to Charles Auger (NCC) for arranging early access to the site.

I am grateful to all my colleagues in the NAU for their advice on aspects of this report, but particularly to Trevor Ashwin and Liz Shepherd for their valuable advice on structure and format of the report, and to Alice Lyons for her thoughts on the pottery. Jez Reeve and Brian Ayers were invaluable for their suggestions on the tone of the report,

for getting the report itself out of my head and onto paper, and for correcting my grammar once it had been written.

I would like to thank David Gurney for his overview and advice on the fieldwork and early analysis stages of the project, and for discussion and his comments on drafts of the report text; I am also grateful for the positive criticism provided by Jude Plouviez and Liz Shepherd on previous drafts.

The Universities Superannuation Scheme, landowners on main excavation site, are to be thanked for their donation of the finds to Norfolk Museums Service; their tenant on the excavation site, Mr Keene, for assisting with early access to main excavation site and providing help whenever it was asked.

The quantities of metalwork and coins from the topsoil were recovered due to the assistance of many local amateurs who worked along side the excavation team: I would like to thank all the metal-detector users and local amateurs who volunteered during the course of the excavation, but particularly John Bocking, who was an ever-present help.

Summary

Part of a Romano-British settlement to the west of the village of Snettisham was excavated in 1989 prior to the construction of the A149 bypass. Although the excavation area was only a small part of the extensive Romano-British settlement in the Ingol valley, valuable information concerning the nature of the activity was recovered.

The excavation revealed that truncated remains of an extensive settlement dating from the mid-first to the late second century survived beneath the modern ploughsoil. The Romano-British settlement was based on a mixed economy of farming and low intensity industry and demonstrated the survival of traditional techniques of house construction, and the continued importance of handmade pottery well into the Roman period. The excavation produced a useful pottery assemblage which complements other groups from the Saxon Shore Fort at Brancaster (Hinchliffe and Sparey-Green 1985), and Fenland sites.

The decline in valley floor activity occurred at approximately the same time as the construction of a villa complex on higher ground to the east, and it is possible that environmental changes in the Fenland region during the third century resulted in the shift of settlement to the east. This eastern focus was also used in the Saxon and medieval periods, and no evidence for intensive post-Roman use of the excavation area was found.

Résumé

Les terres de labour de Snettisham recèlent encore en leur sous-sol quelques traces d'une importante implantation qui s'étendait du milieu du premier siècle jusqu'à la fin du deuxième siècle. Fondée sur une économie mixte, reposant à la fois sur l'agriculture et sur une industrie de faible envergure, cette implantation montre que des techniques traditionnelles de construction de maisons subsistait encore à cette époque et que la poterie faite à la main conservait de l'importance alors que la période romaine était déjà bien entamée. Les fouilles ont permis de mettre à jour un ensemble de poteries d'une grande utilité qui viennent compléter d'autres ensembles provenant du Saxon Shore Fort à Brancaster, et de plusieurs sites des Fens.

L'activité se réduisit dans la vallée environ à la même époque que la construction d'une villa sur une hauteur située à l'est, et il est possible que des modifications de l'environnement dans la région des Fens au cours du troisième siècle entraînèrent un déplacement des habitations vers l'est. Ce changement persista pendant les périodes saxonne et médiévale, et nous ne possédons aucune preuve d'une utilisation intensive de la zone fouillée dans la période post-romaine.
(Traduction: Didier Don)

Zusammenfassung

Teilweise erhaltene ausgedehnte Siedlungsreste aus der Zeit Mitte des 1. Jahrhunderts bis Ende des 2. Jahrhunderts haben unter der heutigen Ackerkrume bei Snettisham überlebt. Die römisch-britische Siedlung, die auf einer Mischung aus Landwirtschaft und leichter Industrietätigkeit aufbaute, demonstriert das Fortbestehen traditioneller Techniken im Häuserbau und die bis weit in die Römerzeit hinein anhaltende Bedeutung handgefertigter Töpferwaren. Die Grabung förderte eine Reihe brauchbarer Keramikgegenstände zutage, die Funde aus dem angelsächsischen Küstenfort von Brancaster und verschiedener anderer Stätten im Fenland ergänzen.

Die Aktivitäten im Talgrund ließen zur etwa gleichen Zeit nach, da weiter östlich eine höher gelegene römische Villa erbaut wurde. Es ist durchaus möglich, dass ökologische Veränderungen im Fenland im 3. Jahrhundert zu einer Siedlungsverlagerung nach Osten hin führten. Die Ausrichtung nach Osten setzte sich in der Zeit der Angelsachsen und im Mittelalter weiter fort. Die Grabungsstätte ergab keine Hinweise auf eine intensive Nutzung in nachrömischer Zeit.
(Übersetzung: Gerlinde Krug)

Chapter 1. Introduction

I. Introduction

The construction of the 5.4km long Dersingham-Ingoldisthorpe-Snettisham Bypass in 1989–1990 followed many years of discussion over its exact course. It was apparent, however, that the road was likely to affect areas of potential archaeological interest and in order to assess the extent of this disturbance the Norfolk Archaeological Unit conducted a fieldwalking and geochemical survey of the proposed roadlines in 1983. This programme identified the section of the road due east of Ingoldisthorpe village as the primary area of interest, where the bypass would cross the apparent site of a Romano-British settlement.

The archaeological response to the road building project was two-fold. A Watching Brief was to be kept on soil disturbance along the whole of 5.4km of the bypass line from TF 683293 to TF 683347; in addition more intensive excavation was proposed to study the 800m length spanning the boundary between Ingoldisthorpe and Snettisham parishes between a track known as 'The Drift' at TF 67888 32455 and the river Ingol at TF 67585 33220. Negotiations between the Unit, the developer (Norfolk County Council), and English Heritage resulted in the Council agreeing to fund the 1989 fieldwork while English Heritage met the post-excavation costs.

II. The Geographical Setting

Geology
The geology of the area comprises part of the Cretaceous Greensand series (white Sandringham Sands, overlain to the east by the loams and clays of the Snettisham Clays, and the ferruginous Carstone) (Casey and Gallois 1973). Trial pits dug on the main excavation site showed that the white Sandringham Sands lay beneath an iron-stained upper zone of sands, covered by between 0.4m and 0.6m of silty grey sand topsoil.

Environmentally the area lies on the edge of a northern extension to the silt skirtlands of the Fens between the Carstone and chalk uplands to the east and the mud flats of the Wash to the west.

Topography
The main topographical feature which the bypass crosses is the broad and shallow valley of the river Ingol which cuts down from the uplands to empty into the Wash. The modern river has been canalised west of Snettisham, and its original course is unknown. Study of Ordnance Survey maps suggests that the parish boundary between Snettisham and Ingoldisthorpe may preserve an earlier course but no trace of a relic stream channel was encountered in the main excavation area and it is possible that the stream ran to the south of 'The Drift'.

The old A149 follows the 10m contour around the base of the escarpment to link the modern villages; the bypass cuts straight across the valley floor, which dips to a little below 5m OD. This route brings it to the edge of the more marshy zone, and this is particularly noticeable at the southern end of the route, where the road cuts through Dersingham Bog, a Site of Special Scientific Interest (SSSI).

The main excavation area lies on a slight south-facing rise on the northern side of the valley floor. The ground rises from around 5.5m to 6.8m OD in the southern 240m of the site, but is generally flat for the remainder. The modern water table was found to be about 1.5m below the field surface, but local information states this is a result of land drainage over the last forty years, and that prior to this the land was very boggy and subject to intermittent upwelling of springs.

III. The Archaeological Background
(Figures 1–3)

The Region
The nature of Romano-British settlement in North-west Norfolk has been discussed by Tony Gregory (Gregory 1982), and subsequent work has not radically altered his description of the area (Figure 1). The area was served by communication routes running north-south and east-west. The Roman road, Peddars Way, ran to the east of the main settlement concentrations towards a probable ferry terminal at Holme next the Sea; the prehistoric communication corridor of the Icknield Way followed a similar route further west, rather nearer to the excavation area, and this route continued in use throughout the Roman period (as the location of the settlements along its length indicates). The east-west road known as the Fen Causeway crossed the fens from *Durobrivae* entering Norfolk at Denver, where it crossed a second north-south route, Akeman Street. This last road's route further north cannot be traced, but it seems to have followed the fen edge at least as far as Shouldham and the River Nar.

Settlement in this area was concentrated along the west side of the chalk uplands, between the chalk and the coastal marshes or fens. Within this band valley-side or spring-line locations were preferred, where a variety of soil-types (and hence environments) could be exploited. The chalk uplands to the east appear to have been less densely settled. This pattern led to a chain of romanised buildings along the chalk escarpment, extending from south of Snettisham to Gayton, 15km away (the seven 'Icknield Way villas' referred to by Tony Gregory (Gregory 1982, 360–366) to which the Snettisham Park Farm villa might be added (Site 1514 on Figure 2). Apart from this last site (with the Ingol settlement to the west and some form of occupation at the head of the Ingol valley at Shernbourne), none of these settlements have provided great evidence for satellite settlements and were interpreted as small estates completely based on the villas themselves.

The apparent lack of luxury on all these sites in West Norfolk may be a result of the marginal location of the area in relation to the social centres of the *civitas* capitals and later to the economic network of 'small towns' that

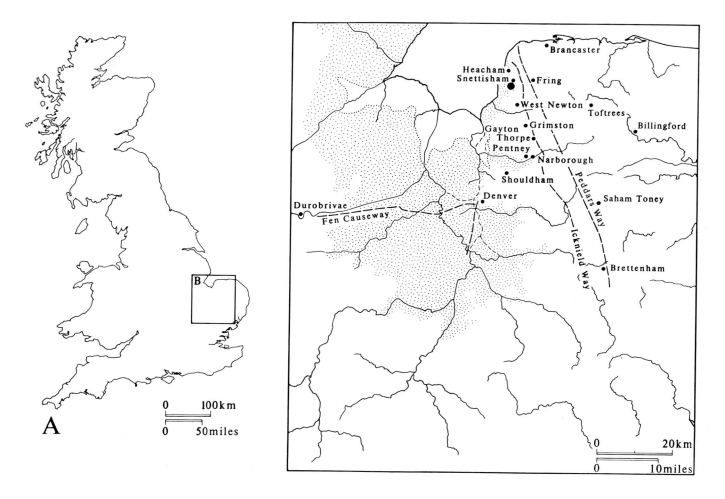

Figure 1 Location of Snettisham

grew up across Roman Britain from the second century onwards. The area lies approximately 70km from the *civitas* capital of *Venta Icenorum* (Caistor St Edmund), and around 30km from the closest of the smaller towns (at Toftrees, Saham Toney, Billingford, and Brettenham— on Figure 1); this latter distance is more than twice that found in other areas (Millett 1990). The cropmark evidence surrounding the Fen Causeway around Denver does suggests a settlement of suitable size to act as a market centre, but there is no evidence to confirm this function.

The Ingol Valley

Study of the county Sites and Monuments Record (SMR) shows that the main excavation area (Site 1555) is situated towards the southern end of a widespread area of Romano-British find-spots. Sites producing Romano-British material are shown on Figure 2; cropmark coverage for the immediate area of the 1989 excavation is detailed on Figure 3.

It appears that much of the northern part of the Ingol valley was under cultivation, with small rectangular fields interspersed with linear tracks (SMR Sites 1515, 18236, 1543, 1554, 1556, 20199, 11829, 28450) and an extensive occupation zone to the immediate east of the main excavation area (Site 1555). Surface finds reported to the county SMR suggest a Romano-British date for these cropmark complexes, but also extend the area of Romano-British activity to the west into the lower-lying marshy area (*e.g.* Sites 1524, 1525, 24583). Although

there is not the density of finds or findspots to suggest that this marks a continuation of the settlement zone itself. The area of occupation appears to have been limited to the north by the slope of Ken Hill: little Romano-British material had been previously found in this area and this impression was not altered during the 1989 Watching Brief on either Site 1544 or Site 1487. The southern boundary of settlement is unclear: Sites 20199 and 11829 indicate that Romano-British cultivation continued to the south of the area excavated, but exactly how far south is not known as no cropmarks or surface finds are recorded in the county SMR for the area south of this. The area was unavailable during the 1983 initial fieldwalking survey, but no new findings were made during the 1989–1990 Watching Brief.

Material recovered from the valley floor sites consisted, in the main, of a range of Romano-British ceramics, brick and tile, coins and brooches; finds of iron slag were also reported from many of the locations, principally those to the north and east of Site 1555. Evaluation of fields to the north of Common Road, Snettisham in 1991 (Site 28450 on Figure 2) demonstrated a similar range of material survived in this north-eastern zone, but also identified metalled road surfaces and two early Romano-British kilns (Flitcroft 1991). These finds were made close to the area which had previously produced the 'Jewellers Hoard' (SMR Site 1517), a collection of gold and silver unearthed during building work, and interpreted as a hoard of waste objects collected for re-use (Potter 1986).

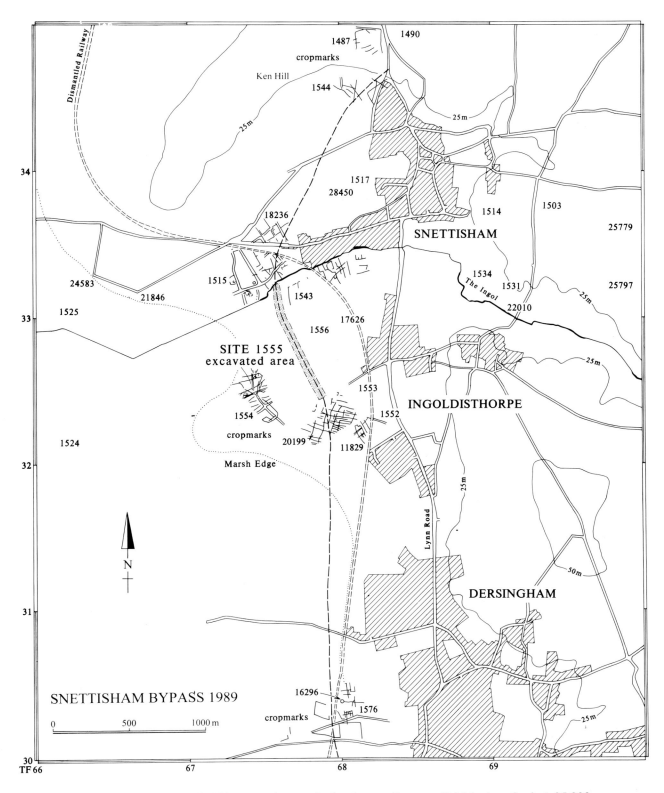

Figure 2 Location of 1989 excavations and other known Romano-British sites. Scale 1:25,000

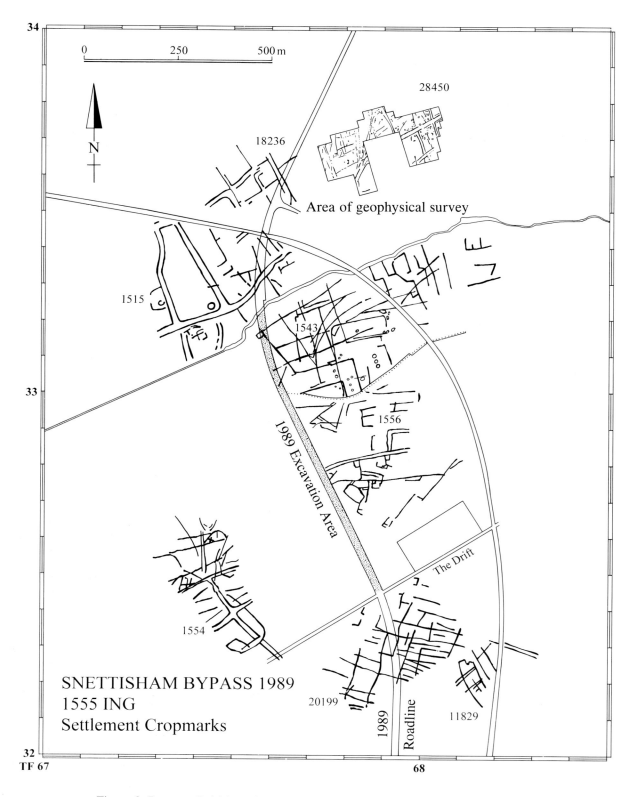

Figure 3 Romano-British settlement cropmarks in the Ingol valley. Scale 1:10,000

4

The discovery of this material provides some indication not only of the geographical spread of Romano-British activity in the Ingol valley, but also its functional diversity.

The eastern boundary is equally uncertain as the modern villages obscure the picture, but the spreads of material found on the slopes and top of the chalk upland to the east of Snettisham suggest that the intervening land may also have been in use. This eastern occupation was centred on the villa at Park Farm, Snettisham (Site 1514) which overlooked the valley from the east. Fieldwalking around this complex has produced further spreads of Romano-British material (Leah and Flitcroft 1993), extending up onto the chalk uplands to the east of the carstone escarpment.

Pre-Roman

Pre-Roman activity in the immediate area of the 1989 excavation seems to have been much less intensive. Neolithic and Bronze Age artefacts have been found on a number of sites apparently concentrated around Ken Hill to the north of the excavation area. Later Iron Age material appears to be more widely distributed, and more common. Metal detecting in the valley floor has produced a small but significant number of Icenian gold and silver coins, further (unstratified) coins were recovered during the 1989 excavations. This period also saw the deliberate burials of groups of precious metal torcs known now as the Snettisham Treasure in the area to the north of the Ingol valley (Clarke, R.R. 1954; Stead 1991).

However the wider region does appear to have been an important focus for activity from the late Bronze Age onwards. Hoards of Bronze Age date have been recovered from Hunstanton, and Shernborne parishes (Clarke, R.R. 1952), and possibly four separate bronze hoards from Snettisham itself. This concentration of metal disposal (for whatever reason it occurred) continued into the Iron Age, culminating (at least in terms of present-day spectacle) in the various Treasure Field torc deposits.

Post-Roman

Saxon finds are restricted again to the upper slopes of Ken Hill, and the main chalk escarpment with Sites 1487 and 1544 producing Ipswich and Thetford Ware pottery, and an early settlement site (Site 1531) being recognised close to the site of the Park Farm villa. Medieval surface finds and sites show a wider distribution, but none of these periods are as well represented as the Romano-British remains.

IV. The Snettisham Bypass Project

Initial field survey of the proposed bypass route, funded by the Department of the Environment, was conducted by the Norfolk Archaeological Unit in the winter of 1983–1984. This comprised fieldwalking, phosphate, and magnetic susceptibility surveys along the two routes then under consideration. The results are summarised in Chapter 2 of this report. This information supplemented work by local metal detector users and previous archaeological work in the area, and identified the main concentrations of archaeological material.

By 1989 the bypass had been given final approval, subject to a Public Enquiry on the affects of the road on the Dersingham Bog SSSI; the Norfolk Archaeological Unit and Norfolk County Council Highways Department had also agreed terms for the archaeological study of the roadline. The final route of the road was to differ slightly from the alternatives surveyed in 1983–1984.

Early access to 800m of the road line from The Drift to the river Ingol was arranged between the County Council and the landowner and tenant, and this area was excavated between July 1989 and February 1990 in advance of the main road building programme. The excavation was conducted by an NAU team of eleven: an Assistant Field Officer, a site supervisor, a finds supervisor, and eight excavators, working under the management of the Unit's Roman period Field Officer. The excavation team was intermittently augmented by local volunteers on the excavation, and by fifty members of local metal detector clubs who conducted an initial survey of the whole bypass line.

When construction of the rest of the bypass began in November a Watching Brief was kept on topsoil disturbance in addition to the continuation of excavation. This Watching Brief continued until April 1990.

Post-excavation analysis of the data from the project, and its synthesis was programmed over a total period of 18 months, which was fragmented by planned (and unplanned) breaks to cover the period from April 1990 to June 1992.

V. Format of the Report

The bulk of this report, including the specialist contributions, was substantially completed by late 1992. Subsequent editing focused on format and content rather than allowing review of the information, and the specialist reports in particular have not had the benefit of reassessment. This report is intended to form a summary of the project, and to act as a key to the full archive report. The approach is intended to be in line with current philosophies on archaeological publication, as outlined by Cunliffe for London (Cunliffe 1990). Although the majority of the project was completed before the second edition of 'Management of Archaeological Projects' (English Heritage 1991) was published, and consequently did not strictly adhere to the model proposed, this report equates to the Published Report described in Appendix 7 and the archive report fulfils the Research Archive role (English Heritage 1991, Appendix 6).

The most noticeable difference between this report-writing philosophy and the traditional Frere 'Level IV' model is the absence of detailed catalogues of finds and corpora of illustrated material. In their place summaries are presented outlining the character of each class of material and its importance to the site and specialist studies.

Appendix 1 contains a full description of the contents of the archive report and the reference system used.

The full site archive, including the archive report, is held by Norfolk Museums Service.

Chapter 2. 1983–1984 Fieldwork

I. Introduction
(Figure 4)

Initial fieldwork was conducted by the Norfolk Archaeological Unit in the winter of 1983–1984 to evaluate the archaeology of the proposed bypass line. At this time the final line of the road had not been decided and two possible routes were surveyed. By 1989 when the road was built a third line was followed, allowing the earlier fieldwork to be used to describe the wider archaeology of the valley.

Three survey methods were used in the evaluation: transect fieldwalking, magnetic susceptibility, and soil phosphate surveying. The evaluation took the form of a single transect walked across all available fields with material collected in 25m units, and soil sampling at the same interval for magnetic susceptibility and phosphate enhancement. Figure 4 shows the results of this work, marking the types of artefact found, and the areas of soil enhancement.

Coverage
All available fields along the two proposed bypass routes were walked, with finds collected in 25m units. To the south of Ingoldisthorpe, where the route coincided with a disused railway track, a line 25m west of the railway was walked. Many of the fields proved unsuitable for walking in the restricted time available for the evaluation because of winter cereal or scrub growth.

The southern part of the route was largely unavailable, and the only field walked was adjacent to the railway, north of the medieval moated site, Gelhams's Manor (SMR Site 1576) in Dersingham parish (shown on Figure 2). The southern area is not shown on Figure 4 because of this absence of coverage. The route in Ingoldisthorpe and Snettisham parishes was walked more intensively. In this area two lines were surveyed, an eastern route following the railway before striking north to pass east of the 1989 excavation site, and a western route which crossed the 1989 site. The two routes had a common northern section from a point immediately south of the Ingol to the slopes of Ken Hill. At this point two further options were surveyed, a southern route passing along the lower slopes of the hill, and a northern which ran across the 'Treasure Field' (SMR Site 1487), where the 'Snettisham Treasure' of Iron Age metalwork was recovered.

II. The Field Survey Results

Fieldwalking
Quantities of pottery, metal production waste, building material and worked flint were found across the whole of the route walked.

Three major concentrations of material were recorded. A spread of Romano-British pottery and slag was recovered from the area south and south-west of the excavation area (Sites 11829 and 20199); the two lines across the excavation site itself (Site 1555) produced large quantities of pottery, slag and puddingstone quern; and Iron Age and Late Saxon ceramics were concentrated on the southern slope of Ken Hill at the northern end of the bypass line. The intervening areas were largely devoid of finds, though small concentrations were recovered between Station Road and Common Road, Snettisham (Sites 20211, 20212, 20214).

Slight scatters of medieval pottery, principally glazed Grimston ware, were recovered from the northern parts of the route, and presumably relate to rubbish disposal from Snettisham village. Worked flint finds were restricted to the very north of the route, on the slopes and top of Ken Hill.

Soil Surveys
by David Gurney

A total of 173 samples were taken from the bypass routes, spanning the area from 'The Drift' Ingoldisthorpe, to the north end of the bypass route. The samples were subdivided for phosphate and magnetic susceptibility analyses. The results are mapped in Figure 4, which indicates areas with readings greater than 2 standard deviations above mean.

The phosphate survey results had a respectably high mean value (91mg P/100g), although this was partly due to a number of very high readings. The standard deviation for the results was 51. The magnetic susceptibility survey results were less clustered having a mean of 191 SI/Kg $x10^{-8}$ and standard deviation of 178. This range may be attributed to the variable nature of the soil matrix sampled, which included dark grey silts and soils with a high organic element.

The soil surveys indicated two main areas of enhanced magnetic susceptibility, believed to be caused by repeated heating and thus possibly indicative of industrial processes. The area immediately north of 'The Drift', to the east of the excavation area (Site 1555) was enhanced to a considerable degree with the highest readings directly north of 'The Drift', and a second smaller peak was recorded to the north of Station Road (Site 20214).

Substantial phosphate enhancement (greater than 1 standard deviation above mean) was recorded over a broad area immediately north of 'The Drift', to the east and south-east of the excavation area with its highest readings towards the centre of the field. A slighter enhancement was recorded further north, to the south of Common Road (marked on Figure 4).

A slight enhancement was noted in both magnetic susceptibility and phosphate samples at the northern end of the bypass where the route ran across the top of Ken Hill (The 'Treasure Field', Site 1487). In this area above-average readings were consistently obtained, though the stronger enhancement noted further south was absent. It is unclear whether this enhancement reflects the archaeology of this field or is a result of different geology, topology or agricultural history.

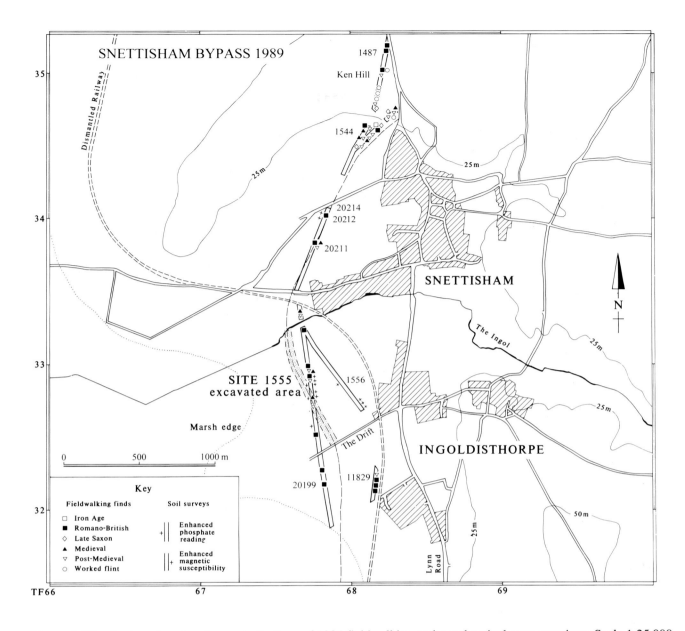

Figure 4 Distribution plot, showing main findings of 1984 fieldwalking and geochemical concentrations. Scale 1:25,000

III. Discussion

The fieldwork identified two main areas of interest: a 1km swathe of land in the valley floor to the north and south of 'The Drift' (SMR Sites 1555, 1556, 11829, 20199, 20200), and a smaller area on the slopes and summit of Ken Hill.

Romano-British pottery of the first three centuries AD was recovered from both areas, and Saxon material was also found on the south side of Ken Hill. The distribution of Romano-British material does not exactly match the evidence from cropmarks and recorded during the bypass construction (discussed in Chapter 6, Watching Brief Results); in particular the area immediately north of the river Ingol (Site 1515) produced no evidence for the extensive remains which were found in 1990.

The soil samples from the Ken Hill area and the southern part of the valley floor concentration did not show any particular enhancement; however the samples from the central part (Sites 1555 and 1556) were considerably enhanced in both surveys. This is an unusual feature, as magnetic susceptibility and phosphate surveys generally produce mutually exclusive high-spots.

The general picture obtained from the fieldwalking and the soil surveys was of spatially extensive activity in the northern half of the Ingol valley (in Ingoldisthorpe and Snettisham parishes) datable to the Roman period, focused in the vicinity of the modern track called 'The Drift', where remains of industrial processes and possibly settlement were concentrated. A second, smaller, area of interest was located on the top and southern slope of Ken Hill where further prehistoric, Roman-British and Saxon remains were noted.

7

Plate I Topsoil removal in progress on Site 1555

Chapter 3. The 1989 Excavation: Site 1555

I. Introduction

An area of 12,000 square metres was made available in July 1989 in advance of the main road construction programme to allow a six-month excavation period. The aim of the excavation was to uncover, assess, and record the surviving archaeological deposits before their destruction. It was decided to strip the whole area under controlled conditions and then selectively excavate parts of the site based on an assessment of the degree of survival and concentration of deposits.

As was mentioned above, the final line of the A149 bypass did not follow either of the routes surveyed in 1983. Instead a 'middle path' was chosen which abandons the existing line of the A149 to the south of Dersingham (at TF 683293) and turns north to cross Dersingham Bog (a Site of Special Scientific Interest), and the disused railway track at TF 679302 to the west of Gelham Manor moat (Site 1576). The bypass continues due north across Dersingham and Ingoldisthorpe commons to the track called 'The Drift' (TF 678324); north of this track it turns slightly to the west along existing field boundaries before crossing the river Ingol and running to Station Road, Snettisham (the area excavated in 1989 extended from 'The Drift' to the Ingol). North of Station Road the bypass line agrees more closely with the original proposed routes, running north-east to the bottom of Ken Hill and then cutting across the hill slope to rejoin the old A149 immediately north of Snettisham village at TF 683347.

The bypass route affected the concentration of Romano-British remains identified in the valley floor during the 1983 evaluation. The area particularly vulnerable was centred on 'The Drift' where Site 20199 was directly affected, and the road would run adjacent to Sites 1555 and 1543.

The evaluation results and aerial photography suggested that Site 20199 was characterised by a network of square fields which had produced no anomalies during the 1983 soil survey, and therefore could provisionally be interpreted as field systems remains. The area chosen for excavation (Site 1555) was selected on the grounds of the concentrations of finds and the magnetic and phosphate anomalies detected in 1983.

A Watching Brief was kept on topsoil disturbance along the whole of the bypass line to record by photography and written record all extant archaeology before its destruction. Limited resources were available for this part of the project, and salvage records were all that could be compiled for most of the line. Through the kindness of the landowners, a survey of the bypass line was conducted by accredited local metal detector users between August and November 1989; this information is considered in conjunction with the Watching Brief results.

Although topsoil stripping was monitored along the whole length of the bypass, archaeological remains were only located in the northern part, and were concentrated immediately north of the area selected for intensive excavation.

II. Site 1555 Excavation Methodology

Initial topsoil removal was made by means of Caterpillar tractor and box-scraper. Soil was removed in spits of c.10 × 2.5 × 0.1m and dumped to the south-east of the excavation area to form a landscape bank. Additional stripping was performed by 360 degree tracked excavator at the northern end of the site (north of Site Grid 760N) and between Site Grid 585N and 600N, where the box-scraper could not easily work because of a farm track and field irrigation pipe. The removal process was monitored by eye and with metal detectors; finds were recovered between each scrape. Small archaeological features were recorded and removed, larger areas protected for later excavation. Unstratified finds were collected in 100m length units, features and associated finds surveyed in to the nearest metre.

Mechanical excavation showed that a grey silty sand layer between 0.45m and 0.6m thick directly overlay natural (though often iron-stained) sand across the whole of the excavation area. This layer is believed to comprise the modern ploughsoil and an indistinguishable thickened subsoil layer. This phenomenon has been noted on other excavations in west Norfolk, including the nearby evaluation at Strickland Avenue, Snettisham (Flitcroft 1991), and at Pott Row Grimston (near Kings Lynn) (Leah 1994). At the latter site Dr Richard Macphail suggested the layer may be a result of intensive worm action, and it is suggested that a similar process may account for the grey soil layer at Snettisham.

Although the majority of features could not be discerned at this level, concentrations of oyster shells, pottery and slag were observed and recorded towards the base of this layer. In retrospect it seems likely that these concentrations marked the upper parts of some of the ditches and pits recorded during the excavation and that the fills could only be recognised clearly where they contrasted with the general grey soil of the area. Soil stripping continued until either the white sand was seen, or archaeological deposits recognised. Although it may have been theoretically possible to excavate a few of these features from their first appearance within the general grey layer, the narrowness of the area available and the importance of establishing the overall layout rather than individual features supports the decision to continue cleaning until the features were widely visible.

As a result of this initial topsoil stripping 'islands' of surviving archaeology were noted. Figure 5 shows all features recorded on the site which were believed to be artificial. The features marked in black represent those recorded during the controlled cleaning and excavation of the site, while those marked as outline only were less certain features — due to extreme truncation or their identification during initial topsoil stripping, when small features were recorded and allowed to be removed). Features recorded the subsequent Watching Brief on mainline road construction in this area are also shown in outline. The site plan and site phase plans (Figures 5, 6,

Plate II Cropmark coverage on Site 1555, to east of excavation area, 18 June 1990
Photograph: Derek A. Edwards (ref: TF6732/AV/GAK10)

Plate III Aerial photograph of Site 1555 during excavation, 4 September 1989
Photograph: Derek A. Edwards (ref: TF6733/AN/DUD10)

26, 37) show only parts of the roadline with surviving stratigraphy; the smaller scale insert in Figure 5 illustrates the entire length of the roadline excavated in 1989. There was a concentration of features between 730N and 780N (recorded as Context Groups 0 and 1 in the archive report) but the area from 600N to 730N proved completely sterile. The main area in which Romano-British features were encountered lay between 370N and 600N (Context Groups 2–7 in the archive), and this was bounded to the south by another area devoid of features. A third island of archaeology was recorded between 160N and 210N (Context Group 8).

Further cleaning by shovel and hoe proved sufficient to define features in most areas of the site, but areas of particular interest were additionally trowelled to increase definition. A number of procedures were adopted in an attempt to accelerate the excavation process: it was decided to concentrate on plans to show the relationships between features rather than the detailed investigation of individual ditches or pits. Plan photographs and area plans were made after the initial cleaning but before excavation, and excavated sections and areas of uncertain stratigraphy were added as they were resolved through additional cleaning and/or excavation. The cleaning was limited to a 10m strip, generally positioned along the centre of the road

line, though this was adjusted where the archaeology encountered required greater width or a realignment to be fully understood.

Areas devoid of features after topsoil scraping (0–180N, 210–370N, 600–730N) were not thoroughly cleaned, as the clarity of features elsewhere strongly indicated that the apparent lack of archaeology was real. Additional confirmation was provided by a sample cleaning exercise in which 10m bands across the excavation area were shovelled and hoed clean every 50m from 0N to 370N to give a 20% sample. The area between 40/605 and 65/730 (between the northernmost group of features and the main area) was stripped by mechanical excavator after box-scraping to locate subsoil features, as concern was raised at the apparent absence of archaeological features in this area. None were noted as a result of the additional stripping.

All but the most minor features were sampled to provide dating evidence, and to aid their interpretation: sub-circular features were half-sectioned, and linear features had 1m sections excavated at intervals. Junctions of linear features had a T-shaped section removed to ascertain their relationship where this could not be easily understood from the surface; it should be noted however, that this was not usually necessary.

11

Ceramic finds were washed and marked on site. More sensitive material was packaged appropriately and sent for conservation, initially at Norwich Castle Museum though much was later forwarded to London University Institute of Archaeology.

Environmental samples were taken from contexts which could be securely related to specific aspects of the site's occupation (such as from house ring ditches and wells) and processed at the University of East Anglia Centre for East Anglian Studies. These comprised both bulk soil samples for carbonised debris and waterlogged samples for pollen and macroscopic analysis.

All contexts were recorded using standardised Norfolk Archaeological Unit recording methods on a sequential numerical series. Unstratified contexts and unstratified finds from cleaning of areas were included. General finds were recorded within their contexts and a separate numerical series established for triangulated and levelled small finds.

During the post-excavation programme these context and finds records were computerised using an in-house Foxbase database application to enable easy access to the information and its presentation.

III. Phasing of Contexts

Due to the nature of the site and the surviving archaeology it proved impossible to construct a strong stratigraphical framework to cover the whole of the site. Although relationships within the individual clusters of features were apparent, the clusters could not be related to each other in any secure manner.

During the post-excavation programme, a provisional site phasing was made, based largely on the stratigraphic relationships between the northern eight clusters of features, which were correlated to provide site-wide phases. It should be clear from this statement that all the features allocated to a particular phase need not have co-existed (particularly when spatially widely-separated features are considered), and it is not the author's intention to imply this. The phases used in this report are, to some extent, purely artificial constructs though they are intended to reflect the major changes in the nature of the site over time.

Phases were identified on the basis of shifts in layout and use of the site, and the presence of structures which could not have co-existed. The relative phasing of each group of features was generally made on the basis of its stratigraphy; phases were linked between the feature groups on the basis of datable artefacts and on alignment of features.

That said, the following arbitrary dating of the phases can be based on the readily datable artefacts (mainly samian and coinage).

Phase 1   mid first century AD
Phase 2   late first century–early second century AD
Phase 3   early–mid second century AD
Phase 4   late second century AD
Phase 5   (late) third century AD

These dates are deliberately broad to reflect the organic nature of site development and the arbitrary nature of the phases themselves. It is unlikely that the small sample excavated would ever permit any greater degree of detail to be included in a discussion of the specific development of individual parts of the site.

Large numbers of features could not be phased. This was particularly true of the deposits identified during the initial topsoil stripping. However it is likely that most of these were associated with the Romano-British settlement, given the paucity of later artefacts and apparent absence of non-Romano-British stratified features.

Chapter 4. Excavated Features

I. Non-Roman Findings

Prehistoric Finds
(Figure 7)

No features were recorded which could be certainly assigned to the period before the mid-first century AD, though unstratified finds hint at prehistoric activity in the general area.

Unstratified finds datable to this long period comprised nine worked flint tools and waste, a Mesolithic stone macehead fragment (Figure 7, No. 2), a Neolithic stone adze head (Figure 7, No. 1), a spear head datable to the Bronze Age — recovered during an 'Open Day' for metal detector users held in September 1989, when the landowner allowed access to the field (Site 1515) immediately north of the 1989 excavation (Site 1555) — and three Icenian gold staters. None of the prehistoric finds came from securely dated contexts.

Post-Roman Features

There was a similar apparent lack of features datable to post-Roman periods, although a large oval pit identified at 590mN (*258* and *294*) and filled with a series of peaty silt layers may be the remains of a post-medieval pond seen on earlier editions of Ordnance Survey 1:2500 maps in this area. It should be noted that the finds assemblage from this feature was entirely Roman in date, which leads to the suggestion that other post-Roman features might be present on the site, similarly invisible. The extent of this mis-attribution is unlikely to be high, given the small number of post-Roman finds from stratified features and from the topsoil and it is more likely to affect the unphased features, which did not conform to the stratigraphic or spatial divisions created.

Finds Summary

Unstratified medieval finds were restricted to a scatter of local glazed Grimston ware from the southernmost 100m of the site. Metal detecting and archaeological monitoring during the course of ploughsoil stripping on Site 1555 produced a small range of the relatively modern metal artefacts that might be expected including horseshoes, fragments of agricultural machinery, and medieval and post-medieval coins.

II. Romano-British Activity: Phase 1 (mid first century AD)
(Figures 6, 8)

As mentioned above, most archaeological activity on the site has been dated to the Roman period, and it is this which will be described and discussed in detail. The discussion will follow a broadly chronological path, with the development across the whole excavated site discussed by phase.

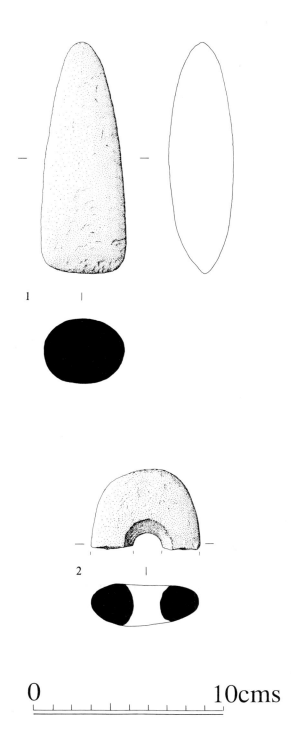

0   10cms

Figure 7 Prehistoric finds. Scale 1:2

Description

In this phase activity was concentrated in the central third of the site, with a structure interpreted as a house (House 1) and a series of enclosures (Enclosures 1, 2) recorded between 470mN and 510mN. Fragments of other ditches were also found, but these formed no clear patterns; the pits, post holes and ditches of this phase are marked in hatching on Figure 6. Phase 1 represents a prelude to the main period of occupation on the site — the limited activity is largely domestic in character, with the extensive field boundary systems of the later settlement apparently absent. The small numbers of finds from this phase are almost entirely ceramic, and these are characterised by handmade forms looking more to Iron Age traditions than to Romano-British influences.

A linear ditch (176) ran north-west/south-east across the northern end of the site (in the area used in Phase 2 for House 2). Associated with this ditch were two large pits (197, 229). All of these were badly cut by the later House 2, and little can be said of their original function. They may be related to activity further north (on Site 1515), but this is little more than speculation based on the apparently early nature of finds on this other site.

A similarly incomprehensible narrow ditch (317) ran partway across the site at 570mN. The zone between ditches 317 and 176 and the area further south produced no evidence for use in this period. This would imply that although some settlement had been established in the locality during this phase, the greater part of the excavation site had not yet been taken into intensive cultivation.

The only part of the site that appears to have been settled at this time lay between 480mN and 530mN. The southern boundary of this zone of small domestic enclosures was formed by a ditch (476) and a gully (474). The area to the south was presumably uncultivated or pasture, although no other land divisions datable to this phase were identified. The northern boundary of this domestic area may have been formed by a flat-bottomed ditch (381) running across the excavation at 530mN. These ditches appear to have formed a stable part of the Phase 1 site arrangement and to have remained in use throughout this phase; the small enclosures and house circle recorded between the ditches were more transitory structures and reflect a piecemeal reorganisation of the existing settlement structure, rather than the complete realignment seen in the later phases of the site. This sequence is illustrated in Figure 8.

The stratigraphically earliest features of this sequence were Enclosure 1 and a small sub-square structure formed by gully 405 (Figure 8.1), a narrow gully enclosing a square area measuring around 4×4m. The gully was cut to the south by the ring ditch of a later building (House 1), and to the north by one of the structural post holes associated with this building; no certain internal features were identified. The function of this gully is unknown, but the similarity in size and profile between it and the wall trench of the later house on the site (410) suggests it may have been a foundation trench for some sort of small square building. Enclosure 1 may have formed a contemporary yard around this structure.

Enclosure 1

The identification of Enclosure 1 is somewhat tentative, and is presented as a possible interpretation of the earliest features in this area.

A gully (392) formed the northern side of the enclosure, curving slightly to the north, where it eventually faded away. It survived as little more than a surface stain, although the same gully may have been recorded to the north of spoilheaps during topsoil stripping as a linear feature (130). Another similarly poorly-preserved gully (414) formed the eastern side of the enclosure. On the basis of alignment only, ditch 476 would seem to have formed the southern boundary of both the enclosure and the whole settlement area. It is possible, however, that at the outset the narrow gully (474) formed the boundary on this line, later removed by the construction of the larger ditch (476). No other certain structures were related to the interior of this enclosure, though it is possible that some of the uninterpreted post holes in this area relate to this part of the site's history.

House 1
(Figures 9–11, Pl. IV)

The square structure (405) was replaced by the construction of a circular building (House 1) within the enclosure (Figures 8.2; 9; 10). The remains of the building comprised a number of structural post holes, part of a wall trench and a later encompassing ditch. The structural elements are shown as shaded features in Figure 9. A fairly regular arc of post holes (423, 450, 452, 440, 446, 447) formed the central circle of vertical posts used to support the roof structure of this house; the ring's diameter of 3.25m and the building's construction is comparable with other excavated examples (e.g. Pryor 1984), but lies at the lower end of the normal range of building sizes.

A curved narrow gully (410) formed the foundation of the outside wall of this house. The gully showed some signs of being dug in sections of around 2.25m in length, which may be related to the hurdles of which the wall was presumably constructed, though no traces of these survived. It has been suggested on other sites that such a wall was likely to have been around 1m high and additionally formed a base on which the roof structure was rested (this hypothesis has been illustrated most clearly in the Little Butser reconstructions). The gully was increasingly truncated to the north and east, and the northern side appears to have been totally removed by ploughing or topsoil stripping.

A second arc of smaller post holes was seen immediately inside the wall gully (518, 519, 522, 719), and these may have formed an additional support for the roof, or have been part of some internal feature.

There were no signs of an entrance in the preserved portion of the gully, and the subsequent construction of an encircling ditch (388) around the house makes it unlikely that an entrance was ever located on the east or north sides where the gully has not survived. It must be assumed that any entrance was located on the west side (as in House 2 in Phase 2) and the apparent straightening of the line of wall foundation and surrounding ring ditch near the west excavation edge supports this. No traces of any occupation layers were recovered from the interior of the building.

Phase 1 Sequence of Structures

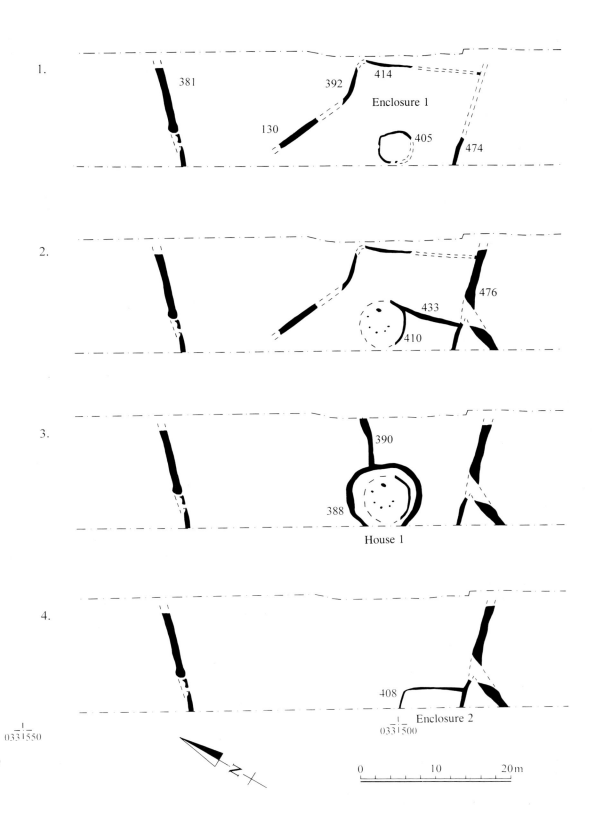

Figure 8 Sequence of Phase 1 structures around House 1. Scale 1:500

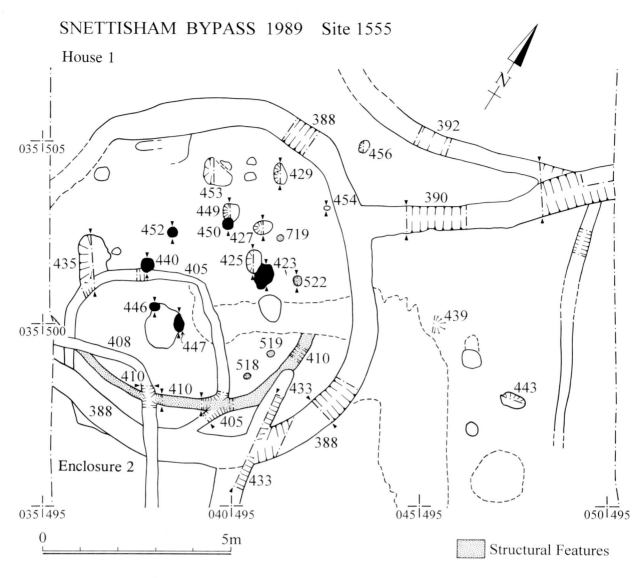

SNETTISHAM BYPASS 1989   Site 1555

House 1

388

392

035 505

456

453

429

449

454

390

452   450

427   719

435   440   405

425   423

522

446

439

035 500

447

408

519

518

410

443

410

433

410

388   405

388

Enclosure 2

433

035 495   040 495   045 495   050 495

0   5m

Structural Features

Figure 9 Plan of House 1, showing structural features. Scale 1:100

Plate IV House 1 before excavation, from north

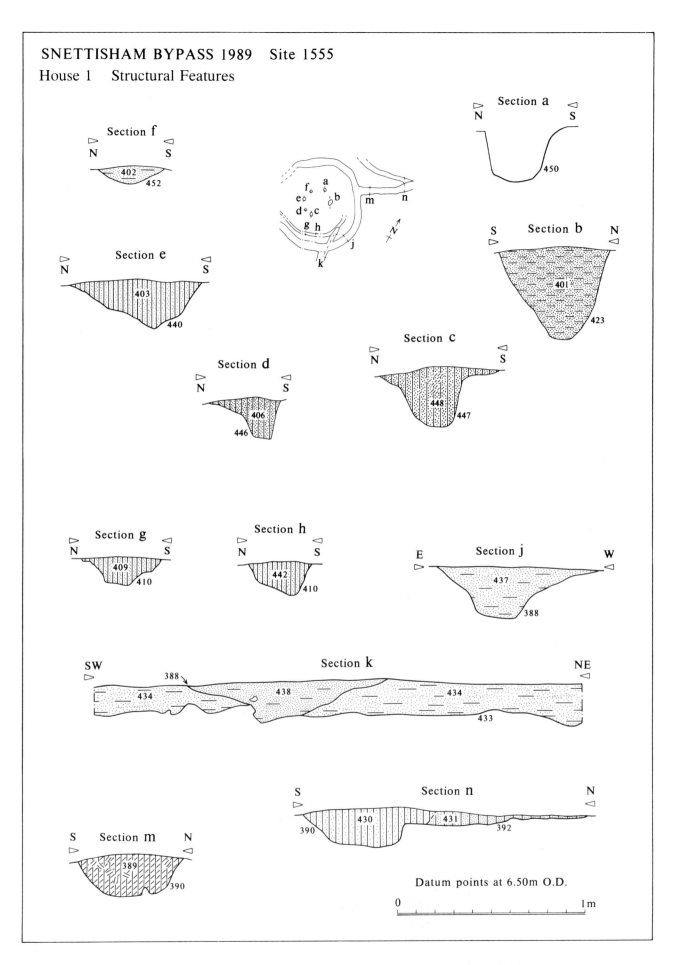

SNETTISHAM BYPASS 1989   Site 1555

House 1   Structural Features

Figure 10 House 1, sections across structural features. Scale 1:20

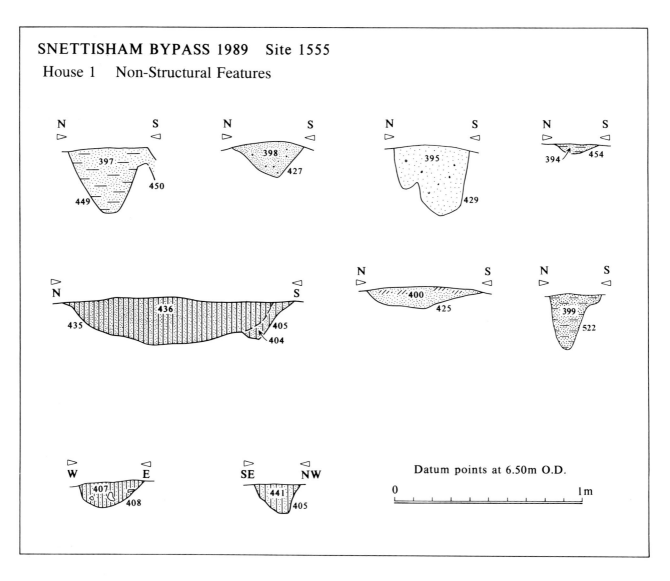

SNETTISHAM BYPASS 1989   Site 1555
House 1   Non-Structural Features

Datum points at 6.50m O.D.

0   1 m

Figure 11 House 1, sections across non-structural features. Scale 1:20

After this house had been constructed the surrounding enclosure was redefined by a gully and fenceline (*433*) running from the edge of the wall trench (*410*) to the southern boundary of the enclosure (Figure 8.2). This created a smaller enclosure with an entrance leading to the north-west along the side of House 1.

Later the area was more fully redesigned and the former enclosure was abandoned (Figure 8.3). The house remained in use and the area was further restricted by the excavation of a circular ditch (*388*) around the house (this cut through the earlier gully (*433*): Figure 10, Section k), and an east-west ditch (*390*). Circumstantial evidence for the short time-lapse between the abandonment of the enclosure and the construction of this ditch is provided by its alignment: the ditch altered its north-eastern alignment to run directly over the corner of the early enclosure. This would suggest that this corner was still visible on the surface at that time; given the minor nature of these two gullies it is unlikely that traces would have survived long after the enclosure was abandoned. The construction of these new ditches (*388* and *390*) produced larger enclosed spaces to the north-east and south-east of the house with the earlier northern ditch (*381*) still forming one recorded

boundary, and the retained southern ditches (*474* and *476*) the other. The house was protected now by its own boundary ditch. This might reflect a change in the use of this area, with the introduction of stock holding to this part of the site and the consequent need to protect the house from animals.

Enclosure 2
This division of the area seems similarly short-lived. The house was soon abandoned and another enclosure (Enclosure 2) was built over its remains (Figure 8.4). The eastern side and north-eastern corner of this enclosure survived in the excavation area as a narrow gully (*408*). This gully ran south to the earlier gully (*474*), which formed the southern side. Enclosure 2 does not appear to have been any longer-lived than the other structures in this area, and was abandoned in the major reorganisation of Phase 2.

Discussion: Finds and Environmental Evidence
Dating individual elements of the house and its sequence of enclosures does not seem to be possible, given the small pottery sample recovered, but reviewing the structure as a

whole it is clear that it was constructed and abandoned before romanised pottery types and fabrics became widespread on the site, placing it early in the relative chronology of the excavation. The presence of (romanised) grey wares in the ring ditch fills may also be taken as evidence that this part of the site does not date to a period much before the rest of the settlement, and a mid/late first century AD date seems likely.

None of the structures produced large numbers of finds. Charcoal was a common inclusion in the later fills; the other finds consisted of small quantities of pottery and animal bone. No evidence was recovered to suggest that any particular craft or industrial activities were conducted around House 1.

The pottery assemblage from the building was relatively small. Although all probable post holes, gullies and ditches were sampled the total number of sherds recovered from structural elements of the building was only 120 (1283g). As with the rest of the phase assemblage, the local gritty R4 was the predominant fabric and was present in all the pottery-producing contexts except one. Fabric descriptions of this, and all other fabrics, are presented in Chapter 6, Section IX. The average sherd size was small, but twenty-three could be definitely said to be from handmade vessels and several of the others may have been from similar types. The size of the sherds makes definition of forms difficult, but one rim sherd from a handmade bowl was recorded in the backfilled ring ditch (388). Decoration on this fabric was limited to eight sherds with burnished or smoothed exteriors.

The only other numerically significant fabric was the sandy R2 (11% by mass), which was only present in four contexts. This fabric appears to have been used for wheel-thrown vessels, though the external smoothing seen on R4 is again present on one R2 sherd, and eight sherds show signs of uneven firing, suggesting that a relatively primitive firing technology was used. Again definition of forms was difficult, but sherds of a possible carinated jar, and another vessel with a flaring rim were noted.

The spatial distribution of the fabrics shows that all the grey ware and white ware sherds, and most of the oxidised fabrics came from the backfill of the ring ditch (388) and the associated enclosure ditch (390). This would suggest a slightly later date of deposition for these fills, which is consistent with the supposed history of this group of features: the ring ditch and enclosure ditch fill would date to the abandonment of the structure, while fills of structural post holes would have been created during construction.

Plant macrofossil samples were taken from four points around the circuit of the circular ditch (388). Analysis of these samples by Peter Murphy has produced a very sparse assemblage of cereals and weed seeds, though some hazel nutshell fragments were also recovered. This assemblage appears to represent a low-density scatter of charred debris from domestic hearths, although the small pieces of slag also noted would imply industrial activity was also being conducted in the area. Ericaceous charcoal is consistently present, and includes some shoots/stems of ling; this could indicate the use of fuel collected in nearby heathland.

The small pottery assemblages were dominated by local Nar valley type products, including a high proportion of handmade vessels manufactured in the Iron Age tradition. The few 'romanised' grey wares recorded were restricted to the fills of the later structures, such as the southern boundary ditch (476) and the house ring ditch (388); the unstratified finds from the initial cleaning over this area produced a similar assemblage (Figure 36). The activity in this area would appear to pre-date the 'romanised' social and trading links that characterised the later phases of the site. The late first and mid second-century samian found in the cleaning layer must be seen as deriving from the later use of this area.

Other Features

The only other traces of activity on the site datable to this preliminary phase were an industrial waste pit (730) at 48/374 and an associated hearth (155) 3m further south (Figure 6), both identified during the Watching Brief on road construction, after the main excavation.

Industrial Waste Pit 730

An isolated pit was recorded in a pipe trench section to the east of the area cleaned for excavation. It was oval in shape with a square hollow cut into its base and contained large numbers of crucible and mould fragments, together with copper alloy wire, slag and first-century samian. A few further crucible and mould fragments were subsequently identified as coming from the initial cleaning in this part of the site. Quantities of both iron and copper slag and charcoal were recorded, and environmental analysis recovered large amounts of eggshell. The mould and crucible fragments were studied by Catherine Mortimer at the Ancient Monuments Laboratory, and parts of three separate moulds were identified (Figure 32.1–3). One appears to have been a possible terret ring mould (Figure 32.1) although too little survived for any attempt at reconstructing the original form; one was an unidentified cylindrical form (Figure 32.2), and the last was a bar ingot mould (Figure 32.3). Three further mould fragments were subsequently identified in the hand-cleaning context from this area (Figure 32.4, 32.5, 32.6). The crucible fragments could not be reconstructed, but x-ray fluorescence indicated they had been used for melting copper alloys. Further details are included below (Chapter 6 Section IV).

The small ceramic assemblage from this feature included single sherds of four of the diagnostic early fabrics OX3, R2 and R4 and R7 (See Chapter 6, Section IX for fabric descriptions), including two jar fragments. Samian from the pit included the earliest dated material from the site, an almost complete (although broken) stamped South Gaulish Form 18R Dish. The stamp on the vessel (of Primus iii, OF(IC, P)RIMI) comes from a known die used at La Graufesenque (3d), and examples of this vessel type have been dated to c.AD55–60 in the Cirencester Fort ditch (Hartley and Dickinson 1982, 120, 35). Part of a South Gaulish Form 30 vessel with possible similarities to a bowl in the Pompeii hoard of AD79 (Atkinson 1914, no. 74) was also recovered, adding weight to the early dating of the pit.

Approximately half a mortarium with a low bead rim and convex flange was recovered (Catalogue No. 31, unillustrated). The vessel had a hard off-white fabric containing sparse quartz, chalk and red iron ore inclusions, and had black slaggy trituration grits. David Gurney, who examined the vessel, provisionally dates it to the second century, and although the source of the mortarium could not be identified, he suggests that it was probably a local product. The (relatively) late date assigned to this vessel is rather at odds with that suggested by the samian, mould and crucible fragments, and other coarse pottery, and it may be that an intermediate date late in the first century would be most likely for the infilling of the industrial pit.

Hearth 155
A roughly circular area of burnt clay interpreted as a hearth was recorded 3m to the south of this pit during the initial topsoil removal. Although it could not be stratigraphically related to the pit its related function suggests it is a contemporary feature.

The presence of this early metalworking dump 120m south of the contemporary enclosures and house, and the east-west boundaries of this northern area suggest that the settlement might have been more extensive in this early phase than might otherwise be guessed from the remains on the excavation site. The 1983 fieldwork and earlier surface finds indicate that Site 1555, the area of the 1989 excavation, lay to the west of the principal spreads of Romano-British material, and it is possible that in this earliest phase settlement had not expanded to cover this area.

III. Romano-British Activity: Phase 2 (late first century to early second century AD)
(Figures 6, 12–15)

Description
An increase in activity is indicated in the late first to early second centuries. Domestic occupation spread to the northern part of the site as well as to the area south of the earlier Phase 1 concentration, and a series of linear boundaries were constructed. These ditches, pits and post holes are marked on Figure 6 in solid black. In presenting the excavated evidence of this phase the general layout of the site is described initially, followed by more detailed treatment of the principal structural elements.

Overall Site Layout
A small industrial waste dump was created at the northern end of the site. Numerous pits (27, 119, 120, 121, 122, 123) formed a compact group of intercutting features (at 59/774), all filled with a silty deposit characterised by large quantities of burnt flint with iron slag and charcoal. This group of pits provides evidence for iron working in the area, though apparently not on the excavated site itself. This activity appears to have taken place inside a large enclosure, visible in aerial photographs as cropmarks to the north and south of the modern course of the Ingol (Site 1515 on Figure 2, cropmarks plotted on Figure 3), the eastern side of this enclosure survived as a ditch (310) within the excavated area of Site 1555. A building complex, comprising a round house (House 2) and small enclosure, was constructed 25m south of these waste pits; this structure would also appear to be inside the large enclosure marked by the cropmarks and boundary ditch (310), although the southern side of this land division was not located during the 1989 excavation. The house is discussed in greater detail below.

The central part of the site was subdivided in this phase by two ditches (308 and 465) curving across the excavated area (between 575mN and 590mN and between 480mN and 490mN respectively). The northernmost ditch (308) had been truncated by ploughing, but survived as a shallow, flat-bottomed feature. A narrow gully had been

dug along its centre to hold a fence line. A second, deeper, ditch and fence boundary (ditch 328) was located just to the south; this feature followed the same alignment, but meandered rather more and may be seen as a redefinition of the boundary.

Further south, the second major feature (ditch 465) was a more substantial boundary ditch than the other and appears to have marked the northern edge of a settlement area. This boundary consisted of a deeper ditch with an asymmetrical profile and no trace of a fence line (Figure 25.1). South of the line of the Phase 1 ditch (476) this boundary became much shallower (Figure 25.3), which may be due to the original existence of a vestigial bank associated with 476 over which this later ditch would have to have risen.

The area between these two boundaries may have formed an agricultural zone, though the presence of an enclosure (Enclosure 3) in this area may imply stock raising or even domestic occupation, and an apparent trackway was identified running north-east along the southern sides of this enclosure. Enclosure 3 is described more fully below.

The area to the south contained features of a more domestic nature. This zone appears to have been limited to the south by two fence and ditch lines (541 and 543; Figure 20). 541 consisted of a narrow asymmetrical ditch with a fence line of post holes in a shallow gully cut into its northern lip. Towards the eastern side of the excavation the fence and ditch appear to separate slightly leaving a narrow strip of natural sand between them (Figure 21.1). The second ditch (543) ran parallel to the other 1.95m to the south. This feature had been badly truncated by a later ditch (588), which followed the same alignment for part of its course.

Features between these boundaries were concentrated towards the southern end of the area. Here a well (Well 1) was dug, with a narrow fence line (715) separating it from the area to the north. (The full history of this well is related below, p.29). To the south-east of the well was a group of at least three intercutting pits (562, 561, 555) covering an area of c.20m^2 (centred on 47/446; Figures 20, 21.3). The material dumped into these pits consisted of pottery, food refuse, and burnt clay including one possible piece of briquetage. The pottery assemblage contained a mixture of handmade local reduced wares and more romanised forms, including cooking vessels and storage jars. These pits were situated just inside the southern side of this occupation zone, and form an area given over to rubbish disposal, particularly of food refuse. Further north was a badly preserved pit (490); this had been largely removed by later features and little could be said of its function. No direct traces of settlement were found, but the well and rubbish pits suggest that buildings were constructed in this area, though not on the excavation line itself; the burnt clay recovered from the pit fills supports this.

The area south of the southernmost boundary ditch (543) produced no features and was presumably in use as fields or pasture in this phase. Any boundary ditches dividing this area had been ploughed out. A final pair of boundary ditches (630 and 623) ran across the site 250m further south. These ditches could not be clearly related to activity on the main part of the site, but their alignment suggests they may have formed part of the same arrangement. Both were badly damaged by plough truncation and later features, and their separation from other areas of archaeology makes further interpretation unrealistic.

Plate V House 2 and enclosure after excavation, from north

House 2
(Figures 12–15, Pl. V)
The surviving elements of the building in the northern part of the site (House 2) consisted of a penannular ditch (*39/101/111/166/195*) with a diameter of *c*.8.3m and a break of 1.3m on the western side; the northern side of the circuit was overcut during machining but survived as a soil stain. This ditch would appear to have functioned as a boundary rather than being a structural element of the house itself, although truncation of the site had removed almost all traces of the superstructure from this house. Due to mechanical problems with the topsoil stripping operation in the period immediately after this structure was first identified (and the consequent impossibility of work elsewhere on the site) it was possible to excavate virtually all the surviving parts of the house, rather than simply representative samples.

The house had a west-facing entrance; four post holes (*250, 252, 256, 280*) and the possible remains of a hearth (*271*) were all that remained of the original interior. Two of the post holes (*252* and *256*) appear to have been aligned parallel with the entrance, and it is possible that they held internal supports; other evidence for supports in the entrance area may have been removed by a later pit (Phase 3, Pit *87*). The other two post holes could not be interpreted from the little that survived.

Immediately south of the building was an enclosure ditch (*42/93*), which enclosed an unusually small area of only 4.2m × 5.4m. Terminals of the ditches were found 3m and 2.25m south of the outer edge of the house, and it seems very unlikely that this ditch was not directly associated with the hut circle, particularly as matching breaks were found among the pottery dumped in the ring ditch and enclosure ditch during the abandonment of the complex. Along the east arm were a number of possible stake holes (*202, 204*) cutting through the lower fills of the ditch and overlain by the loam backfilling. These may have formed a palisade along the base of the ditch, but the absence of similar features in the western arm, and the degree of animal and root disturbance in the upper fills make it possible that this was the cause of these holes. No traces of any internal features were found and the writer cannot suggest a likely use for this enclosure. It would appear to be too small for any stock-keeping purpose, and it seems very unlikely that its area was further restricted by any form of internal superstructure. A broadly similar small enclosure was recorded associated with an Iron Age round house at Vince's Farm, Ardleigh, Essex (Erith and Holbert 1970), though this example was considered to have formed an earlier alignment of a larger enclosure surrounding the round house.

One further feature which may have been associated with the occupation of this house was a dog burial (*40*) lying 3m west of the southern end of the small enclosure. It was not possible to relate this feature directly to other features in this part of the site, but the inclusion of two sherds of first-century South Gaulish samian in the backfill of the grave may suggest an early date.

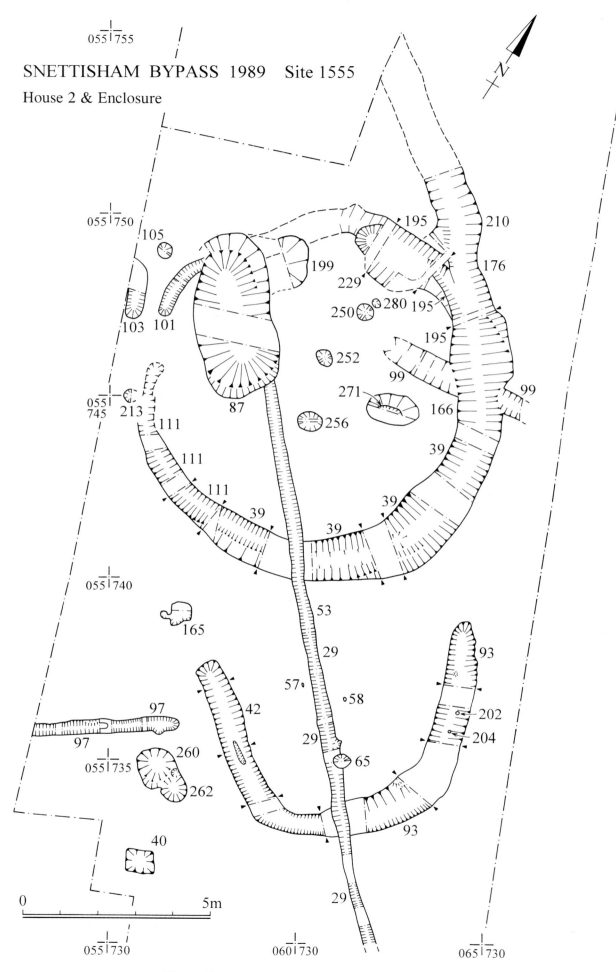

SNETTISHAM BYPASS 1989   Site 1555

House 2 & Enclosure

Figure 12 House 2 and associated enclosure. Scale 1:100

24

SNETTISHAM BYPASS 1989   Site 1555
House 2

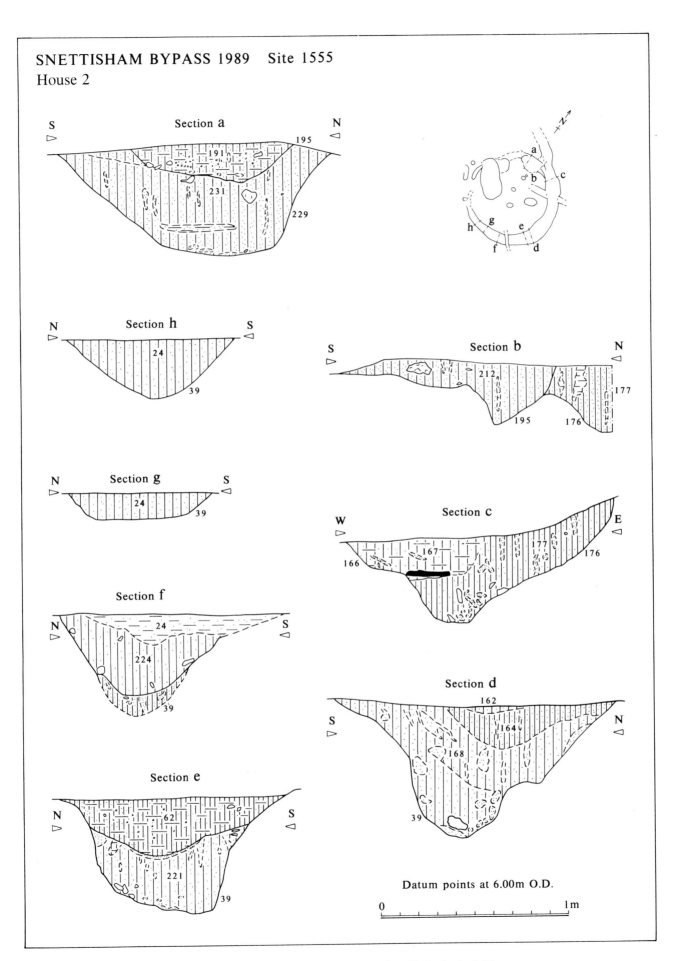

Figure 13 House 2, sections across ring ditch. Scale 1:20

SNETTISHAM BYPASS 1989   Site 1555
House 2 Enclosure

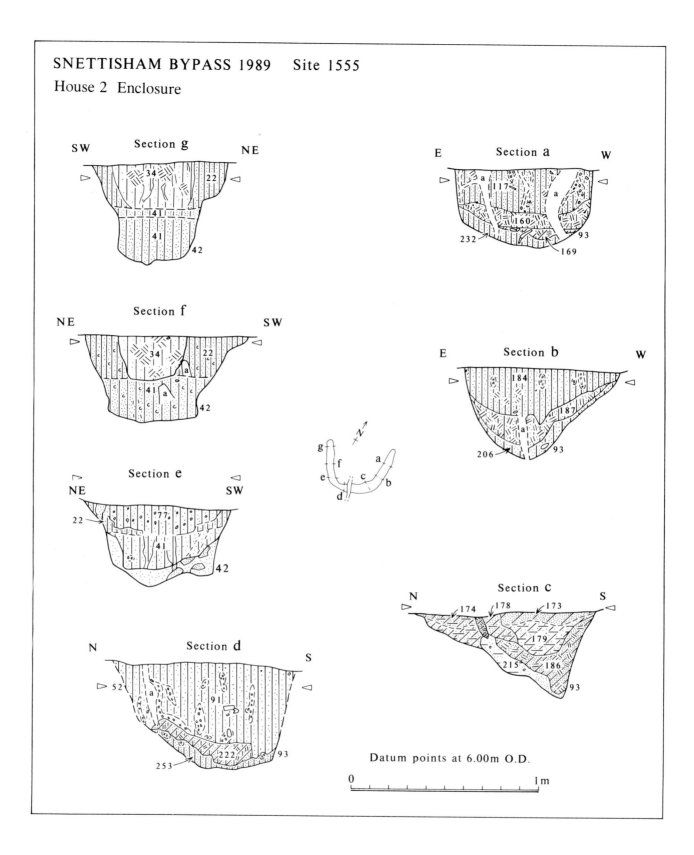

Figure 14 House 2, sections across enclosure ditch. Scale 1:20

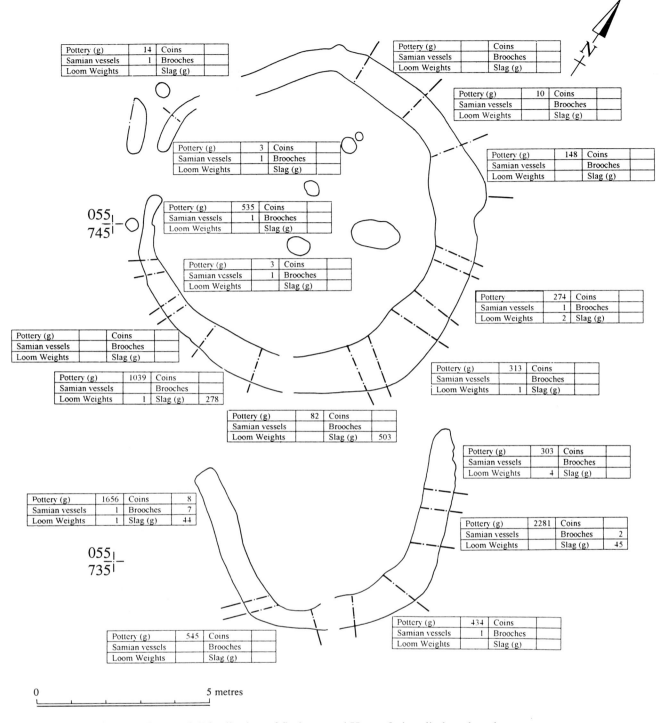

Figure 15 Distribution of finds around House 2 ring ditch and enclosure

During the backfilling of the small enclosure ditch (42/93) a mass of burnt rubbish material was deposited in the east arm, and burnt clay/daub, presumably from the superstructure of the house, was also found in the backfill of both ring ditch and enclosure. The distribution of the material (shown in Figure 15) has a marked concentration towards the southern side of the structure; this may be partly due to truncation of the north-west part of the ring ditch, but the scarcity of finds in the deeper deposits in the north-east quadrant suggests that this is also a reflection of the original deposition pattern. This distribution and

quantity of material suggest a deliberate final dismantling of the structure and a levelling of the site, rather than abandonment and a slow decay which would have scattered this burnt rubbish, and may indicate that the building survived until the area was reorganised (Phase 3). A second phase of backfilling was seen in the western arm of the enclosure, and the sharp edges to this visible in section (Figure 14) imply a second cut in this area, a cut which may not have been directly associated with the building and enclosure but which may relate to another phase of activity on the site.

27

The evidence from the abandonment of this complex suggests a number of craft and industrial processes may have been undertaken around the building: loomweight fragments in the backfills of both house and enclosure suggest weaving, though the scale of this cannot be gauged; the slag recovered from all parts of the backfill points to iron working in the area. A dump of six brooches in the western arm of the enclosure with a further two on the east side and one in the ring ditch fill, were initially believed to be a jeweller's stock, but the absence of any crucibles or other bronze-casting debris, and the broad range of types present has subsequently led to the hoard being interpreted as the loss of a personal jewellery collection, either inadvertently during demolition of the building, or potentially in a deliberate action. All these brooches are datable to the middle third of the first century; a further seven similar brooches were recovered during initial topsoil stripping from this general area. The brooches are illustrated and described below (Chapter 6; Figure 30). The samian found in the same backfill contexts was found to have a slightly later date range than the brooches, with material from the last quarter of the first century extending into the early second century. This date range is supported by the coarse pottery assemblage, with diagnostic 'early' fabrics forming the main constituents while not including the high proportion of handmade types seen around the earlier house (House 1, Phase 1). The ceramic date-range adds weight to the interpretation of the brooch hoard as a jewellery collection, as such items might be expected to have remained in circulation longer than individual losses before becoming part of the archaeological record.

The ceramic assemblage from House 2 included examples of twenty-three different fabrics, although the eight most significant fabrics (numerically) accounted for 80% of the total. The main fabrics represented were the hard grey ware G2 and the sandy reduced type R2. The sandy oxidised fabric OX3 was numerically also significant, but this appears to be affected by the small size into which sherds were broken.

The form range (Figure 37) included types of jars, bowls, beakers, flagons, dishes, and storage vessels. Grey ware jars were the most frequently identified form, with twelve examples from the ring ditch fill, and thirty-five from the enclosure ditch. Bowls were generally restricted to the reduced fabrics, and flagons to the oxidised. Four sherds of three separate beakers were found in the enclosure ditch fill (three sherds from two vessels in *187*, a fourth sherd of another vessel in *179*).

Decorative techniques represented in the assemblage consisted largely of external scoring — either created on the wheel to form horizontal lines, or free-hand. A band of lattice decoration is found around the shoulders of a small proportion of the grey ware vessels, and a related rouletting technique is evident on single sherds found in the enclosure ditch fill (*42*) and the ring ditch (*167*). One other decorative fashion used relatively widely on storage jars and flagons in the local fabrics R4 and OX4 involved combed lines in panels around the shoulders or extending over the entire vessel body. Rusticated sherds were also recorded, and this technique was again restricted to the locally produced R4 and black-surfaced OX1 fabrics.

The coarse ware assemblage appears typical of the early-middle phase of the site, with the 'early' fabrics (OX2, R4) present in reasonable quantities, although

surpassed numerically by the romanised wares (such as G2, G5 and OX3).

Externally datable ceramics from House 2 consisted of mortarium fragments and sherds of samian. Three sherds of a Brockley Hill mortarium with a stamp dated *c*.60–90AD were recovered from the lower backfill of the enclosure ditch (*42*; Figure 35, No.1). This part of the enclosure ditch fill also produced a concentration of Flavian samian (although other similarly early sherds were found throughout the enclosure ditch). The ring ditch also produced early samian, including a matching break with the enclosure ditch. Parts of at least twelve separate vessels were recovered, with Forms 15/17 or 18, 18, 18/37, 27, 36, and 37 represented. The assemblage incorporates vessels individually dated as Neronian/early Flavian, and Flavian, and to the period 79–95AD; all datable vessel fragments came from the lower fills of the enclosure and from the house ditch.

The coins from the backfill of the complex extend beyond the immediate period suggested by the ceramic and brooch finds, ranging from an obviously antique republican issue to four coins of Antoninus Pius (138–161AD) and one of Caracalla (207AD). However all the coins were recovered from the later fill of the enclosure ditch (*42*), and their later date adds weight to the suggestion made above that the second infilling of the enclosure ditch may not be directly associated with the currency of the building.

The quantity of material recovered from this house and its enclosure was far greater than might be expected, even allowing for the larger proportion which was excavated; and the quality and nature of the goods was also notable for this site. It appears that when the building went out of use little effort was made to recover the portable artefacts, such as the numerous brooches, the relatively large number of samian vessels represented, or the loomweights (many of which were still usable). There are no readily apparent explanations for this: although there were charcoal deposits, particularly in the enclosure fill, few of the objects are burnt and conflagration should be discounted; the lack of any real pattern in the distribution of the artefacts within the complex suggests that it was not some form of termination ritual of the type discussed by Merrifield (Merrifield 1987, 49).

Enclosure 3
The south-east and south-west sides of this enclosure were formed by three ditches (*354, 378* and *426*). Another ditch fragment (*352*) might form part of the north-east side, but this is not certain. The only features that could be related stratigraphically or spatially to the interior of this enclosure were a group of pits (*372, 383, 420*) dug against its southern side and used to dispose of domestic waste including a further three brooches broadly similar in type to those in the House 2 backfill. This group was also analysed by D. Mackreth and the brooches identified as one Colchester type (typologically dated to the early–mid first century), and two Colchester Derivatives (possibly dating to the mid-first century). The brooches were considered to be more worn and less complete than the other group. This degree of wear may have been the reason for their disposal in the refuse pit.

Well 1

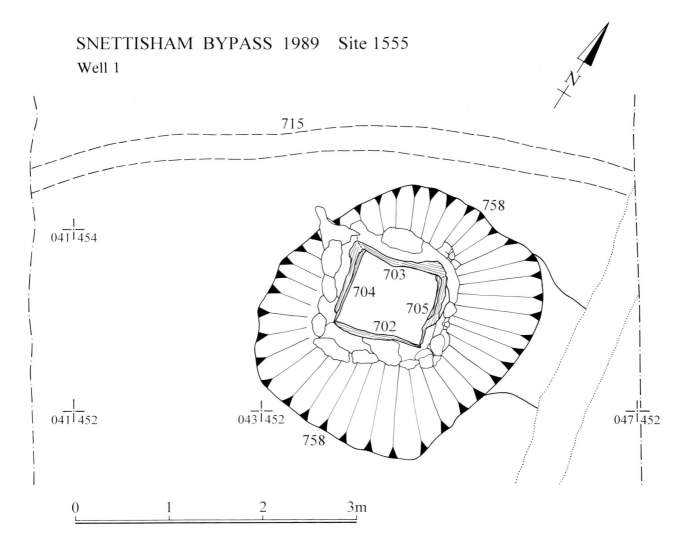

Figure 16 Plan of Well 1

Well 1
(Figures 16–18, Pls IX, X)
The construction of this well has been assigned to this phase on the basis of the feature's relationship to other features and its apparent period of use, as no finds were recovered from deposits associated with the construction phase of this structure.

A roughly circular pit was excavated down to water table, and a square wooden lining inserted into its base. This lining used the tangentially split outer parts of a single oak tree trunk to make an open box joined at the corners with half-butt joints without use of nails (Figure 17). The timbers were submitted for dendrochronological dating, but insufficient growth rings were present to allow dating. Only one course of timber was found during the excavation, but at least one further course can be presumed from the continuation of the packing on the southern side of the well pit (visible on Figure 18), and the presence of slighter planks in the initial backfill suggests a light-weight lining nearer the top of the shaft. Structural stability was achieved through the size of the timbers used at the base of the shaft, and their external packing with quantities of stone. After this wooden lining and packing had been inserted, the construction pit was backfilled with loam. The well remained in use throughout Phase 2 and may have continued until the end

Well 1

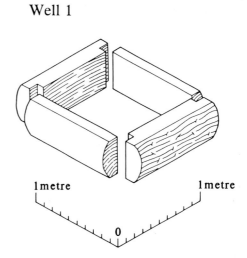

Figure 17 Isometric reconstruction of Well 1 lining

of the second century. No traces of well superstructure were recovered although it could be seen that the structure was separated from the area to its north by the construction of a slightly curved fence line (*715*).

Well 1

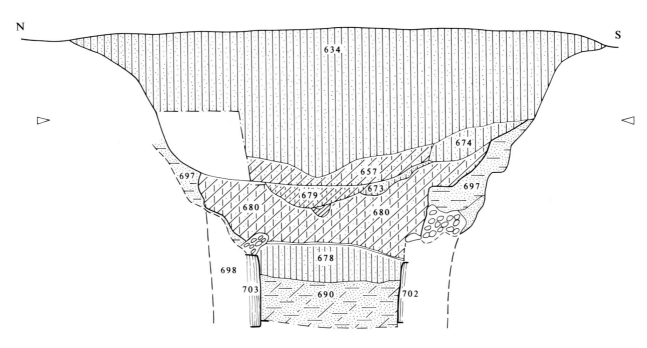

Well 2

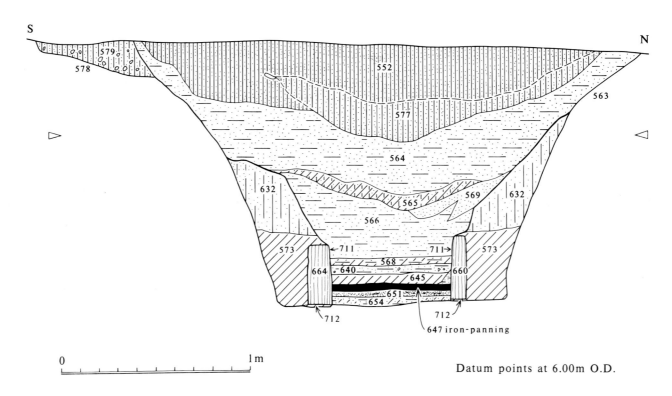

Figure 18 Sections across Wells 1 and 2. Scale 1:20

Datum points at 6.00m O.D.

IV. Phase 3 (early–mid second century AD)
(Figures 19–27)

The third phase of activity saw the nature of the site changing, with ditched trackways running across it (between 605mN and 580mN and between 410mN and 396mN). Between these major divisions a series of small enclosures was created, and although no buildings were directly associated with these structures, the remains of wells and a crop-processing area strongly suggest their presence in the immediate area. The ditches and pits assigned to Phase 3 are marked on Figure 19; the black features identify a slightly later reorganisation of the central area of the site, but this should still be seen as part of the Phase 3 layout.

Description
There was a marked change in the nature of the activity at the northern end of the site after the removal of the earlier building (House 2; Figure 12). The domestic occupation of Phase 2 was replaced with linear divisions of an open area: the site of House 2 was divided by fence lines (29 and 97), and a water storage pit (87) was dug. Three hearths (272, 279, 281) were constructed to the north.

The longest length of fence (29) survived as a shallow U-profiled gully running from pit 87 south-east towards the excavation edge. Four small circular features were cut into its base, but their excavator could not be certain that they were not sugar beet tap roots, and so they have not been used as evidence for the fence itself. The other fence (97) was aligned at 90° and ran west into the excavation edge, leaving a gap of c. 3.7m between its eastern terminal and other fence; the gullies had similar dimensions and fill. There were no stake holes in the second gully, but two possible post-settings were found. These two fences formed the east and south sides of some type of stockade enclosure, with an entrance leading south.

The small pits (260 and 262) immediately south of one fence (97) and a post hole (65) on the line of the other (29) may have held posts related to this entrance (Figure 12): although the fills of all these features show no evidence for the survival of posts this may simply be due to their later removal. It should also be noted that identifiable post-pipes were a very uncommon find over the whole site, as the silty soil and general absence of stones tended to produce homogenous fills.

The large subrectangular water storage pit (87) at the north end of one fence (29) had a bowled profile and contained an apparent lining of grey silty clay with a compacted surface. This lining would have helped to retain water and it is suggested that the pit was used as a reservoir situated at the edge of the fenced enclosure. The alignment of fence and pit indicate that both were planned parts of this stockade. The fence was not observed to the north of this pit, but this may have been due to the greater truncation of the site in this area. It seems clear from the unabraded pottery and burnt clay recovered from the fills of fence gully 97 and the daub from the large pit (87) that occupation continued in the immediate area after this reorganisation of the site, but that natural shifts in settlement had left the area of the modern roadline free of housing.

To the north of this pit, and outside the presumed enclosure, three oval hearths were built (272, 279 and 281). The similarity of all three and their grouping suggest they were all built for the same purpose, and the presence of slag in the backfill of one of these hollows suggests their use as ore roasting hearths. A rectangular pit (738; Figure 5) seen to the west of these hearths during the Watching Brief on road construction contained more slag, including a hearth bottom, and charcoal deposits. This should be considered to be part of the same industrial processing centre. A shallow ditch (99) was also recorded on the eastern side of the excavation area, and aligned on the large pit (87). This feature had been badly truncated, and its function could not be defined.

Trackway Ditches 245 and 285
A pair of ditches (245 and 285) ran across the site (between 605mN and 580mN) with a separation of 4.4m. These formed the two sides of a trackway or droveway between fields, although the original surface of the track had not survived. The lack of contemporary features either north or south of this track suggests this part of the site was given over to arable production in this phase. This land division appears to have been maintained over some time, as the northern ditch showed signs of two episodes of partial silting followed by recutting. The southern ditch does not show the same sequence, but this may be simply due to more vigorous recutting.

The ditches were finally backfilled with a series of small dumps of loam and general domestic rubbish, which included some fragments of a first or second-century cylindrical blue/green glass bottle (catalogue No. 5). Relatively large amounts of coarse pottery were dumped in these ditches, with a wide variety of vessel types and fabrics represented.

The northern ditch (285) mainly contained the sandy grey ware G5 and the sandyish R2. Other material comprised G2 and R1, a handmade vessel rim in fabric OX6, and a bowl form in the speckled G3. The southern ditch (245) had a larger, more diverse, assemblage. The smooth hard G2 fabric was predominant, although reasonable amounts of R2 were also recovered from the upper fill. All the main oxidised fabrics were present in the assemblage. The primary fill produced both handmade and wheel-thrown jars in the local gritty R4 fabric, illustrating the continued use of these local sources. The size of the assemblage and the numbers of linking sherds imply that when these ditches were filled the opportunity was taken to dump previously discarded breakages. The material ranged from local handmade storage jars to thin-walled jars and bowls with rouletted decoration, though fairly coarse cooking jars were the most frequently occurring form.

Three sherds of Nene Valley Grey Ware datable to the second half of the second century appear to be the latest material in the assemblage, though the numbers of handmade pots looking to Iron Age traditions and the complete mixing of wares throughout the backfill layers suggest that these Nene Valley wares are simply the latest component of a long-term rubbish pile that was used to fill these ditches. The complete absence of samian from such a dump is remarkable and cannot easily be explained.

Trackway Ditches 571 and 575
A second pair of drove/trackway ditches ran across the southern part of the site (between 410mN and 396mN). Two ditches (571 and 575) marked the sides of another c. 4m wide trackway, though again no trace of any surface survived. This track appears to have had a similarly

31

extended lifespan, though it may not have been in continuous use as the southern ditch (575) showed evidence of backfilling followed by recutting slightly to the north.

Evidence for a fence line along the northern lip of the northern ditch (571) was found, while to the south of the southern ditch circumstantial evidence pointed towards the presence of a narrow bank. Although no traces of such a bank survived in the excavation, the truncation of a contemporary gully (596) to the south of the trackway ditch implies it had risen up at this point to climb some form of bank flanking the trackway. This gully (596) was interpreted as forming a division of the fields to the south of the trackway because of its alignment. The construction of the northern fence line may have occurred in the mid second century. The small assemblage from a post hole fill included a sherd of Trajanic samian, and while dating based on single sherds cannot be reliable the lifespan of the ditch and the dating of its backfill suggest this may be a reasonable date for the construction.

This drove/trackway appears to have been finally removed and the ditches filled in the latter part of the second century. The pottery assemblage was smaller than those recovered from the northern trackway ditches, with roughly similar ranges of fabrics and forms from the two ditches (571 and 575). The assemblage contained a mixture of sandy reduced ware, R2, orange OX3 and the common grey ware G5 with forms represented including several flagons (fabrics G5, OX3, OX4, W5) and jars (largely in fabric G5), and sherds of a strainer/cheese press (fabric R4; Figure 39 No. 41). Several handmade burnished vessel sherds were also recovered.

The residual nature of some of this material is suggested by a greater number of abraded sherds, the absence of large numbers of linking pieces and the recovery of a single fragment of South Gaulish Form 18 samian datable to the Neronian or early Flavian period from ditch 575. A single sherd of Nene Valley Grey Ware from ditch 596 supports the later second-century date.

The area south of this trackway appears to have been used for agriculture in Phase 3, with the only contemporary features being the internal boundary ditch mentioned earlier (596). The area to the north, by contrast, was given over to domestic occupation, characterised by crop processing structures and small enclosures. When the ditches were backfilled this domestic and processing aspect was reflected in the ceramic assemblage, with cooking vessels, flagons and the only cheese-press/strainer fragments from the site coming from these deposits.

Enclosure 4
(Figures 20 and 21)

A trapezoidal enclosure (Enclosure 4 on Figure 20) was built 10m further north into this occupation zone, with its southern side parallel to the trackway ditches, and a narrow entrance in its south-western corner. The western side of this enclosure was formed by a ditch (589), and could be traced running north (to 447mN) before appearing to turn to the east. The southern and south-eastern sides were formed by another ditch (578).

A well (Well 2) was dug into the corner of this enclosure, and Figure 20 shows that it was clearly an intentional part of this structure as the enclosure ditch curved closely around the edge of the well shaft, becoming erased when the larger well demolition pit was dug. The earlier well further north (Well 1) also appears to have continued in use throughout this phase.

After a period of use Enclosure 4 was abandoned, and the boundary ditches backfilled with topsoil. Environmental analysis of the sediments from the well inside this enclosure (Well 2) suggests that it remained open at this time while the surrounding area became increasingly overgrown with weeds (this aspect is discussed more fully below in the description of Well 2). The small coarseware assemblage from the abandonment of this enclosure reflected the domestic nature of the structure. All the pottery appears to be redeposited refuse: some of the sherds were heavily abraded, all of them were small fragments. The only vessels recognised were two bowl rims, and part of a white flagon. This assemblage could not, in itself, be dated but the period of decay observed in the fills of the well suggests that the ditches of Enclosure 6 were backfilled in the second half of the second century AD, before the trackway ditches were abandoned.

Well 2
(Figures 18, 22, 23, Pl.VI)

A roughly circular bowled pit was dug down to the water table and a box of interlocked planks was dropped onto a sealing layer of yellow clay. The box was made of radially cut oak planks joined with half-depth lap joints to form a square box with external wings (Figure 23). These wings would have become earthfast supports for the wooden shaft after the construction pit was backfilled. All the timbers recovered were submitted for dendro-chronological analysis, which indicated that the trees from which they had been cut were probably felled sometime between 100 and 145AD, the uncertainty being due to a lack of sapwood and bark from the timbers. Remains of two courses of well lining were found and it appears that the individual jointed boxes were not fastened to each other in any way, although the seams were sealed with clay. The construction cut was backfilled with clay and sandy loam, but as with the earlier well (Well 1), the later dismantling had removed the upper courses of the shaft, and nothing can be said of any superstructure.

A period of use followed, before the surrounding enclosure was abandoned and its boundary ditches filled. Well 2 was allowed to decay at this time and began to silt up naturally with a series of thin bands of deposit forming in the still open shaft (Figure 18). The gradual marginalisation of this area is reflected in the plant remains identified in the environmental samples from the lower fills of the shaft. Nettle was the predominant species in all the samples, but increased in abundance over time. The silting process may have begun before the abandonment of the well, as the lowest layer contained wood chips presumed to be from the construction phase.

After a period of time, in which 30mm of silt had formed in the open well, it was decided to recover as much of the timber lining as possible and level the site. A conical pit was dug through the backfilled enclosure boundary ditch and the well construction fills and the lining removed to the depth of the silted shaft. The pit was backfilled fairly rapidly with topsoil, though a slump of natural sand was interleaved with this.

removed until the latter part of the century, giving a total lifespan of 40 or 50 years. Of this time perhaps half related to the use of the well and half to its decay. Well 2 was dismantled during the reorganisation of this part of the site which marks the boundary between Phases 3 and 4, when another enclosure (Enclosure 7) was created and the adjacent land was required.

Two further enclosures were also created during Phase 3 (Enclosures 5 and 6; 40m north of Enclosure 4), and are shown in Figure 24 with sections on Figure 25. The southern boundary of both these features was formed by a ditch (*514*) which seems to have held a palisade. This ditch appears to have marked another division of the site comparable to the fenced ditch described earlier (*571*), separating domestic occupation — marked by Enclosure 4, and the two wells — from a zone of small enclosures, possibly used for industrial processing, to the immediate north.

Enclosure 5
Enclosure 5 was bounded within the excavated area by three ditches (*462*, *488* and *514*). These had been badly truncated and were discontinuous in places. The southern side (*514*) was the best preserved, with some evidence for post settings along its base. Its stratigraphical relationship with the eastern side (*488*) had been removed by the later ditch *757*.

Enclosure 6
After parts of Enclosure 5 had become at least partly backfilled a new enclosure (Enclosure 6) was built to the east which utilised the original east side of the earlier enclosure (*488*) as its western limit, retaining the palisaded ditch (*514*) as its southern limit. This continuity of boundaries between the two enclosures suggests little or no break in occupation between these two structures.

Few features could be associated with the interiors of either enclosure. Two pits (*503* and *490*) might have been dug inside the earlier enclosure, but both were cut by a later ring ditch (House 3), and little can be said of their original function. No internal feature could be associated with Enclosure 6. However, a concentration of six possible iron-processing hearths were recorded in this area during initial topsoil stripping, and it is likely that they are connected with these two enclosures.

The enclosures were replaced (Phase 3B on Figure 19) by a broader single ditch (*757*), which preserved the line of the former southern boundary (*514*), and by the construction of a house (House 3, below). These features mark a change of use of the area north of the boundary, with the enclosures and their possible industrial use being replaced by domestic occupation. However the continuity of the southern boundary suggests that these changes were less important than the later, more wholesale, replanning which formed Phase 4.

House 3
A curved ditch (*495*; Figure 24) formed the western half of a ring ditch around House 3, analogous to the ditch (*388*) around House 1. The ditch was badly truncated, and no internal structural features of the building were seen; it was interpreted as a house ring ditch solely on its diameter.

Unlike Houses 1 and 2 in the first two phases, this structure did not appear to have a west-facing entrance; the entrance presumably lay to the north or east since the structure was flanked by a ditch (*757*) to the south. The eventual backfilling of the ring ditch (*495*) included five small, heavily abraded body sherds in fabrics OX4, OX5, and R2, and a very abraded scrap of rim in fabric R7. No diagnostic fragments were recovered, and little further can be interpreted from the assemblage.

Corn Drier 144
(Figures 26, 27, Pl. VII)
A corn drier (*144*) was constructed in the 'processing zone' suggested between Enclosure 4 and the trackway ditches to the south (*571* and *575*). The allocation of this structure to Phase 3 is admittedly somewhat arbitrary; although it is only in this phase that activity becomes widespread in this part of the excavated area.

The first structure consisted of a south-facing T-shaped flue constructed of packed clay (*590*). Use of the drier resulted in the partial firing of the floor of this flue, and environmental samples taken from charcoal deposits over the floor (*535*) contained a high proportion of sprouted wheat grains, characteristic of malt-drying ovens. After a period of use the corn drier was rebuilt on the same foundations to the same plan. A stoking hollow and chalk floor were created at the north end of the structure and the T-shaped flue rebuilt using clay blocks (*526*). The outlines of some of these blocks can be seen on Figures 26 and 27, where they have become separated by infilling soil.

Continued use resulted once again in the partial baking of the flue floor (*527*), and the deposition of a charcoal layer (*528*). Environmental analysis of this deposit revealed a different composition from the lower charcoal layer. Spelt chaff predominated, with seeds of common weeds, wood charcoal and a few wheat grains. A full description of the assemblage is provided in the Archive Report (Section 5.4, Table 2). This was interpreted by Peter Murphy as the remains of various cereal byproducts used as fuel for the drier. Eventually the corn drier was abandoned and the stoking hollow filled with a mixture of unfired clay and loam (*542*).

Many pieces of the sandy reduced fabric R2 were recovered during initial cleaning over the corn drier; these have been interpreted as fragments of the drier superstructure, given the coarse nature of the matrix and the lack of curvature. Pottery sherds were more scarce around this feature, but four sherds (fabrics R2, R4, R7, OX3) of 'early' fabrics were recovered from the matrix of corn drier *144*; none is illustrated.

The function of so-called 'corn driers' has been much disputed, but Van der Veen (1989) reviewing the available evidence has indicated that consideration of the nature of charred plant remains assemblages may aid interpretation. The relatively large number of charred sprouted cereal grains in the lower deposit may be taken as evidence for malt drying during this phase of the structure, whereas the presence of chaff and few cereal grains in the upper deposit are likely to represent fuel residues rather than the material being dried.

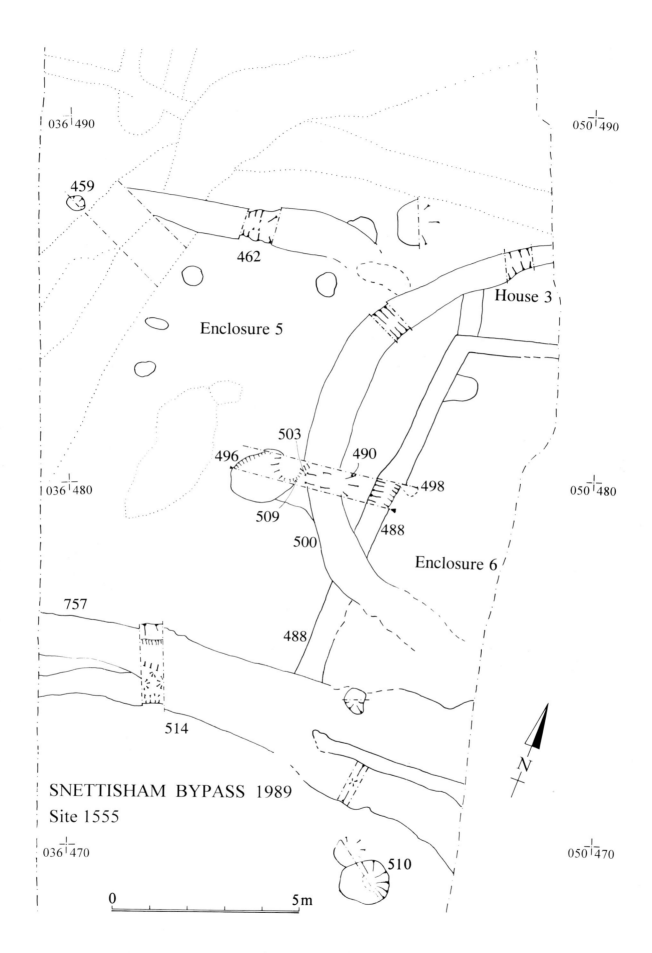

036⎯490

050⎯490

459

462

Enclosure 5

House 3

503

496

490

509

498

500

488

Enclosure 6

036⎯480

050⎯480

757

514

488

SNETTISHAM BYPASS 1989
Site 1555

036⎯470

050⎯470

510

0   5m

N

Figure 24 Plan of Enclosures 5 and 6, and associated features. Scale 1:100

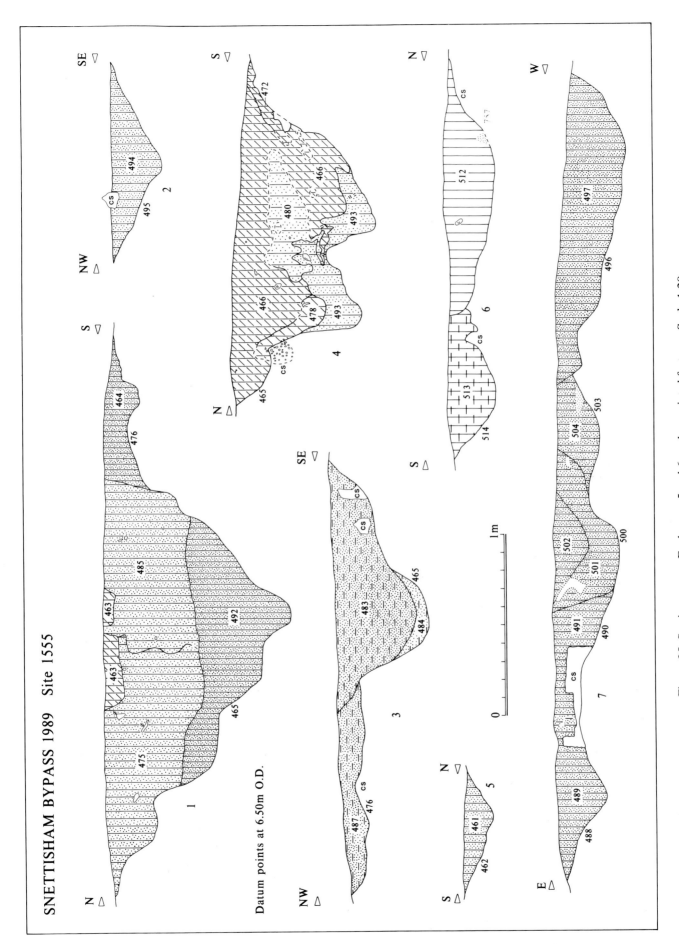

SNETTISHAM BYPASS 1989   Site 1555

Datum points at 6.50m O.D.

Figure 25 Sections across Enclosures 5 and 6, and associated features. Scale 1:20

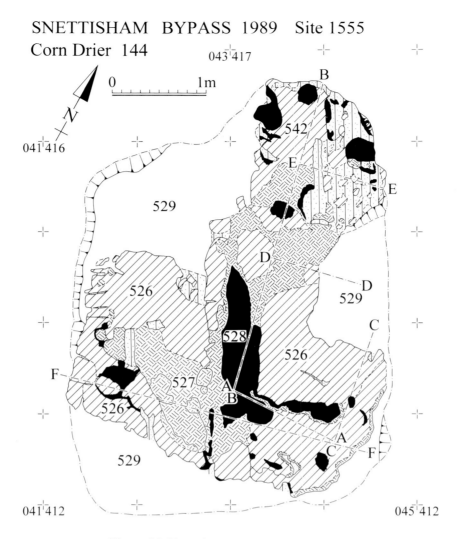

SNETTISHAM BYPASS 1989 Site 1555
Corn Drier 144

043'417

0   1m

041'416

B

542

E

E

529

D

526

D

529

C

528

526

F

527   A

B

526

A

529   C   F

041'412   045'412

Figure 26 Plan of corn drier *144*. Scale 1:40

Plate VII Corn drier *144*

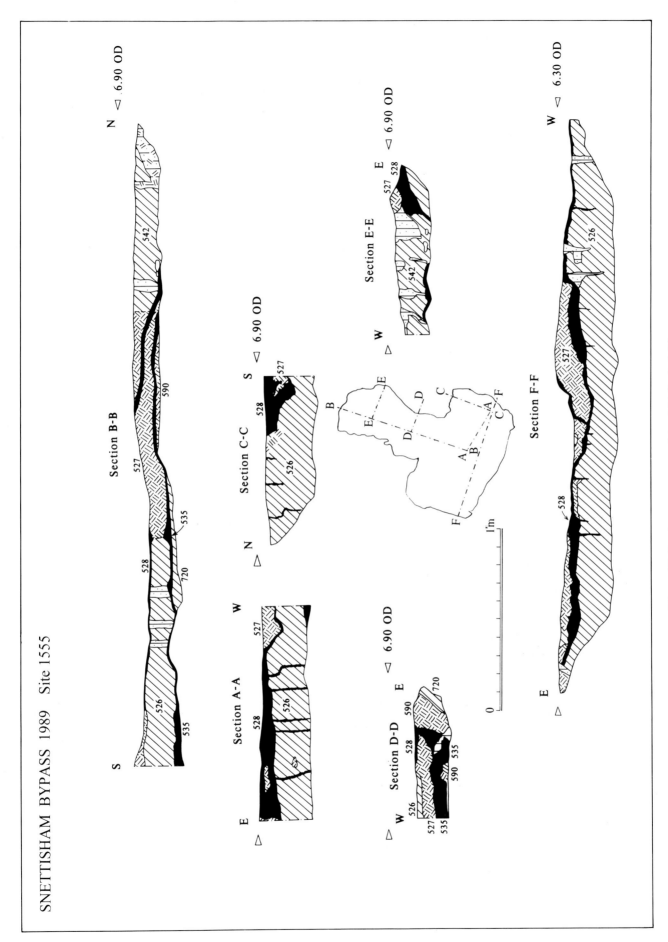

SNETTISHAM BYPASS 1989   Site 1555

Section B-B

Section A-A

Section C-C

Section D-D

Section E-E

Section F-F

Figure 27 Sections across corn drier *144*. Scale 1:20

41

V. Phase 4 (late second century AD)
(Figure 28)

This phase marks the abandonment of the land divisions and settlement pattern of Phase 3, and its replacement with a lower density of activity. The ditches and pits of Phase 4 are shown in hatching on Figure 28.

Description

The northern 200m of the site were devoid of features relating to this or the subsequent phase. This might be explained by use of this area for large fields, though the area north of the river Ingol (Site 1515) also produced no real evidence for occupation in this later part of the site's history, and it is possible that a field-based system of agriculture was abandoned in this whole northern area after the later second century.

Trackway Ditches 274 and 297
The area of the earlier northern trackway ditches (around 600mN) seems to have continued in agricultural use as a new ditched trackway was created, running north–south at right angles to the Phase 3 track (*245/285*). Two truncated ditches (*297* and *274*) marked the sides of a track around 5m wide running across the site. No trace of a track surface survived and the flanking ditches were shallower than the earlier ditches. The land either side of this track appears to be empty of structural features and would appear to be a continuation of the open area discussed above.

When this track went out of use it was backfilled with general topsoil containing a small pottery assemblage (48 sherds, 284g). Some of this material was abraded and single sherds of mid first and mid second-century samian indicate that some must be residual. This pottery is probably redeposited material from the earlier settlement in the area which had been responsible for the larger assemblage in the previous trackway ditches. Fragments of a Central Gaulish Form 27 samian bowl were also recovered. This form can be dated to the mid second century (not illustrated).

Enclosure 7
The only area in which some activity appears to have continued on the site is much further to the south (immediately south of 450mN) where Enclosure 7 was created to the east of Enclosure 4 (Phase 3). The eastern and northern sides of this enclosure (*588*) lay within the excavation area and their alignment with earlier ditches (the eastern with Phase 3 ditch *589*, the northern with Phase 2 ditch *543*) suggests that some earthwork traces of these boundaries remained. The presence of the only grave on the site immediately east of this enclosure suggests it may have marked an outlying part of a settlement centred further west, rather than an agricultural enclosure. The presence of several externally-sooted pottery sherds in the eventual backfill of this ditch also suggests that it was part of a domestic enclosure. Excavated sections in the southern part of this ditch produced evidence for a fence line in the base, but further north this does not seem to have been the case, and a simple ditch formed the boundary.

Parts of three samian vessels were recovered from this enclosure ditch (*531/588*): These comprise a South Gaulish Form 18 datable to the Flavian period, a South Gaulish Form 30, and Form 37 bowl both datable to the mid/late first century.

Plate VIII Inhumation *548*, from south

Grave 549
(Pl. VIII)
A single grave was dug 2.5m east of this enclosure (Grave *549* on Figures 28 and 20), and its alignment with the enclosure edge suggests it may have been dug while this enclosure was in use. The inhumation (*548*) was that of an elderly male buried in a supine position with his head raised on a step cut in the base of the grave and his feet hard up against the south end of the grave (Plate VIII). The only grave good buried with him was a single globular beaker placed beside his head (Figure 41 No. 52). The significance of this single burial to the history of the site is uncertain. Inhumation became the more common funeral rite from the mid second century onwards, but the significance of an (apparently) single grave on a rural settlement cannot be gauged until further research in this part of the region identifies other burial customs.

Other Features
The southern well (Well 2) to the east of this enclosure and grave was abandoned at this time. A demolition pit was dug to recover much of the timber lining, and the pit was filled in with bulk layers of silty sand and loam. Peter Murphy's analysis of the environmental samples from the northern well (Well 1) suggests it may also have been abandoned and overgrown with nettles at this time, but it does not appear to have been dismantled until later.

A minor division of the site was formed by a gully (*598*), 20m south of Enclosure 7. This boundary may have separated the zone containing Enclosure 7 from the area to the south and it is tempting to suggest that Enclosure 7

Plate IX. Well 1, showing details of lining

Plate X Well 1, dismantling of timber lining

Other Features

To the south of this well were two small pits (*713, 600;* Figure 20). The southern pit (*600*) cut the backfilled ditch of Enclosure 7 (Figures 20, 21.4) and was filled with layers of sandy silt, producing numerous small pieces of burnt clay although no datable finds. The northern pit (*713*) was smaller and filled with a dark brown sandy loam fill. A further small pit (*607*; 65m to the south) was also dug at this time. Its clay-loam fill produced a single small pottery sherd. A gully (*677*) ran north to south to the immediate east of the well and appeared to cut through its upper demolition fills; this feature was badly truncated and was only traced for a short distance.

The northern pit (*713*) produced the only other artefact assemblage from this phase; coarse pottery from this feature comprised sherds of nine different fabrics, principally the hard grey ware G2, but including two Nene Valley Grey Ware sherds. Rim fragments of two bowls (a flared bowl in fabric G2 and a plain Nene Valley Grey Ware rim) and a jar (Fabric G4) were identified; a flagon body sherd (Fabric W4) was also noted. None of this assemblage was large enough to be illustrated.

The presence of daub and roof tile fragments in the well backfill and the lack of other characteristic 'late' artefacts from the area around the excavation may suggest a wider abandonment of the settlement, with 'romanised' tiled buildings being demolished and the material transported to the excavation area to level the site.

Chapter 5. Watching Brief Results

I. Introduction

A Watching Brief was kept on topsoil disturbance along the whole of the bypass line, and the results of this complemented the initial fieldwork undertaken in 1983–1984 when the bypass line was first planned. Both of these studies permit the wider interpretation of the excavation area.

Although all parts of the bypass line were monitored after the removal of topsoil, areas of archaeological remains were only encountered in the area immediately north of Site 1555, the main excavation (Figure 29).

II. Watching Brief Methodology

The original aim of the Watching Brief was to observe all construction work involving disturbance of the topsoil and record by photography and written/drawn record all archaeological deposits *in situ* before destruction.

Due to the number of concurrent topsoiling operations this proved to be impossible without committing so large a proportion of the excavation team that work faltered on Site 1555. Accordingly it was decided to concentrate on deposits revealed after the removal of unstratified topsoil, before they were obscured by passage of construction traffic. This was achieved by outposting one or two people from the excavation team each day to inspect all works along the bypass line.

The one area which was made an exception was the northern end of the bypass. Here the road ran along the south side of Site 1487, which had produced the Snettisham Treasure (a collection of Iron Age jewellery), and it was decided that it would be prudent to monitor topsoil removal more closely in this division. Two archaeologists were present throughout all soil removal operations in this area, and each load of soil was monitored as it was removed.

Inspection was generally limited to collecting surface scatters of material and surveying in soilmarks, but in the area directly north of the river Ingol (Site 1515), salvage excavations were required to recover dating evidence from the larger number of deposits revealed. These took the form of measured area plans with spade-dug sections across major features.

Features recorded during the Watching Brief were located by reference to the chainage markers surveyed as part of the bypass construction. Contexts were given individual numbers as part of the excavation sequence in the field, starting at *2048*, and these were correlated against the county-wide SMR context number series during the post-excavation stage; a few contexts were not given county site numbers because of their natural origin.

Recording was made on standardised Norfolk Archaeological Unit sheets, though in less detail than for stratified contexts on the excavation site, supported by photographs and plans as required.

III. Watching Brief Results

Full details of the Watching Brief findings are included in the Archive Report (Section 3), presented by SMR Site code. Syntheses of the main findings are included here, discussed in a north to south sequence along the bypass line. Single ditches, of uncertain date, were encountered 600m and 400m south of the excavation area (Site 25752), and fairly recent building foundations recorded 800m north of the site (Site 25750, described below).

Sites 1487, 1544
(Figure 2)

The northern terminal of the bypass line was monitored more closely than other parts of the route, as it passed to the immediate south of the field in which the Snettisham Treasure had been deposited. In this area the roadline was to be embanked at the base of the hill and a cutting made at the top, and consequently while large quantities of bedrock were removed from the top of the hill, little more than turf removal was conducted at the base. No structural evidence was found in this area, but metal detecting recovered early second-century and third/fourth-century coins from the base of the hill (Site 1544).

The topsoil at the top of the hill (Site 1487) produced no Iron Age or Romano-British material, though quantities of medieval Grimston earthenware were found. This was presumably the result of rubbish dumping from the medieval village of Snettisham.

Site 25750
(not illustrated)

At a point approximately 800m north of Site 1555 a building complex of relatively recent date was recorded. The complex consisted of two pits, and two sub-rectangular areas of sand and chalk pebbles providing foundations for two small structures each measuring approximately 8 × 4m. No finds were recovered from the building foundations themselves, but the pits produced medieval glazed Grimston pottery and modern butchery debris, and the complex would appear to be post-medieval in date.

Site 25751
(not illustrated)

A concentration of brick rubble was encountered approximately 400m north of Site 1555; fragments of modern blue-and-white glazed pottery give this feature a relatively modern date.

Site 18236
(Figure 2)

Although aerial photography suggested that further parts of the Romano-British valley floor settlement might be encountered in this area, the Watching Brief produced no evidence for the survival of linear features.

Site Plan

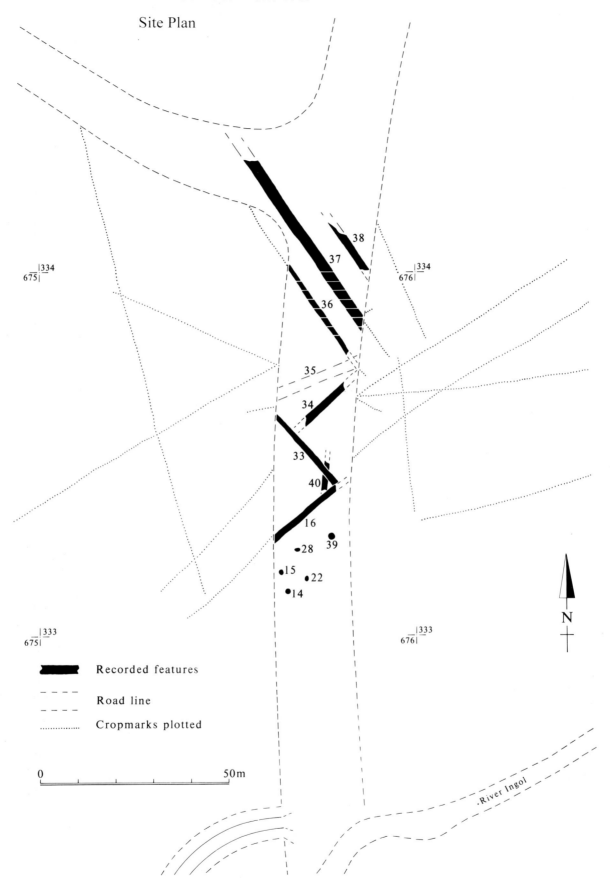

Figure 29 Site 1515, site plan. Scale 1:1000

Site 1515
(Figures 2 and 29)

The only place in which extensive areas of archaeology remained was immediately north of the main excavation (Site 1555), on the opposite bank of the modern course of the Ingol. This area also had cropmark coverage and had been previously fieldwalked, and the excavated features correlated reasonably well with these. Figure 29 records the location of all the features seen on this site, with cropmarks plotted as dotted lines. The features here had to be recorded quickly, and a salvage record was all that could be made.

Description
(Figure 29)

Two ditches (*16* and *34*) formed the sides of a major trackway running between fields and enclosures, with two others (*36* and *37*) marking a subsidiary lane running off this track. The other ditches recorded (*33, 38, 40*) could not be related to the cropmark pattern, and appear to be a later reorganisation. The area south of the major track (*16/34*) may have been used for industrial processes as five small pits (*14, 15, 22, 28, 39*) were recorded on the roadline in this area, and their fills produced slag and pottery wasters. The infill of the southern major track ditch (*16*) also suggested pottery manufacture in the southern part of this field, with large numbers of partially complete vessels and wasters being recovered. The pottery assemblage from these ditches was comparable with that from Site 1555, although wasters were only found on Site 1515. Samian and mortaria from the ditch suggest this production was centred in the mid second century, which again compares well with the results from Site 1555.

Finds Summary: Site 1515

Apart from Site 1555, this part of the bypass line was the only area to produce significant quantities of material. Most of it was recovered during the salvage excavations and provides an interesting complement to the artefacts from the main site.

Brooches
by D. Mackreth

A total of four complete brooches and one additional fragment were recovered from this site. The complete examples were all recovered from the fill of Pit *22*. The assemblage comprises three Colchester Derivatives (Figure 31, Nos 4, 8, 10), one unclassified type (No. 24), and a fragment of a bent pin with two sheet pieces forming part of a circle (No. 36). The brooches are described in greater detail in Chapter 6.

The Colchester Derivative examples are similar to those found on Site 1555 in using a rearward-facing hook as the chief visible means of securing the spring. This is considered to be a specifically Icenian style of the mid first century, being restricted to northern East Anglia and consistently dated to the period *c.* 40–60/65 AD (Mackreth 1996).

Samian
by B. Dickinson

Samian was recovered from most features on Site 1515 and the assemblage spans the period from the mid first to the later second centuries AD. Parts of at least twenty-five vessels were recovered, with South Gaulish Forms 15/17, 18, 27, 36, 37, Curle 11; Central Gaulish Forms 18/31R, 31, 33, 37, 38, 81 and East Gaulish (La Madeleine factory) Form 27 represented. A full descriptive catalogue is included in the Archive Report (Section 4.7).

Mortaria
by David Gurney

Parts of five mortaria were recovered from the fills of trackway ditches *16* and *34* on Site 1515. Four of the vessels are likely local products from unidentified kilns, having a cream/yellow fabric containing very sparse quartz and reddish-brown inclusions and flint and/or quartz trituration grits (Archive Report Nos 34, 35, 36, 38). The fifth vessel (Figure 35, No. 33) is more interesting, being of a different fabric and also stamped. The stamp is clear enough, but not entirely straightforward to interpret. It is likely that the name Crescens is intended. One potter's stamp survives and two others are recorded, both from Baylham, near Ipswich. There is a good possibility that he worked at Baylham, and the rim-forms leave no doubt that he was active in the period AD 60–90 (K. Hartley pers. comm.).

The date range of these five vessels is uncertain, but appears to cover the period from the mid first century (No. 33, above) to the second century. The fabrics represented are very similar to those from Site 1555, and it can be assumed that mortaria were made at the same ?East Anglian workshops. A full descriptive catalogue is included in the Archive Report (Section 4.8).

Amphora
by D. Williams

Sherds from at least four vessels were recovered (none illustrated). Examples of Dressel 20, Gauloise 4 and a ?Gallic type were identified.

Pottery
by M. Flitcroft

A total of 12.4kg of coarse pottery was recovered during salvage excavations on Site 1515, almost all of this identified as Romano-British material. As the site was excavated under adverse conditions and no phasing of the contexts was possible, the pottery has been considered as a site total and not subdivided in any way.

The range of fabrics present is very similar to that on Site 1555, with the gritty local reduced ware R4, and the grey wares G2 and G5 being the most common. No Nene Valley wares were identified and this, taken in conjunction with the absence of later vessel form types, may indicate an earlier cessation of activity in this part of the settlement.

Forms include types intuitively considered as early Roman, such as campanulate bowls; types similar to the Iron Age style handmade vessels found on Site 1555 are absent. Other vessel types include a range of jars, and bowls and folded beakers in local reduced fabrics — similar vessels were found during an evaluation of a kiln site 700m east (Site 28450) within the same settlement zone (Flitcroft 1991). Decoration consists of external burnishing, scored lines, rustication.

Some evidence for pottery production was noted in the identification of wasters (or at least 'seconds') with sporled surfaces, and overfired vessels. These include an R2 bowl (Figure 43, No. 69) and a G2 jar (Figure 43, No. 68), and overfired flagon (and undiagnostic) sherds in O4.

Site 20199
(Figures 2 and 3)
It was anticipated that Romano-British features or artefacts would be encountered during the Watching Brief on this site, as surface finds and cropmarks had been observed, but very few features were recorded, either on the roadline itself or in a borrow pit dug to the south. The features visible in this pit did not form part of the general field system, and were partly of more recent date.

Chapter 6. Finds Summaries

All artefacts from Site 1555 and the Watching Brief were subjected to analysis at differing levels of intensity. Specialist contributions were generally completed and submitted by late 1992, and have not been consistently updated to reflect subsequent research. The full texts of these reports form part of the archive report (Archive Report Section 4), but summaries are included here. It is intended that these summaries will allow an assessment of the value of the full text for any particular research.

I. Iron Age Coins
by Tony Gregory
(Archive Report Section 4.1)

Three coins were discovered by metal detectors during the 1989 excavation: an Icenian gold stater, British Na of the latter part of the first century BC; a silver unit of Pattern-Horse type, likely to have been produced in the second or third quarter of the first century AD; and a gold quarter-stater of previously unrecorded type, equivalent to British Ja (Norfolk Wolf) (Plate XI). The obverse of this last coin showed (off-centre) a curved crest-like motif with curls at edge; the reverse showed a wolf-like animal (facing right). By analogy with the full denomination this quarter-stater should probably date to the mid first century BC.

Two others were found earlier, some distance to the east, though near enough to be regarded as from the same general site (two gold staters of Gallo-Belgic Type C, unpublished but entered in the Index of Celtic coins at the Oxford Institute of Archaeology, datable to the early part of the first century AD).

Although the sample is small it is interesting: four of the coins are early, pre-dating the issue of silver, an unusual circumstance which is normally reversed. It is difficult to escape the conclusion that coins were in use in this area in the first century BC.

II. Roman and Later Coins
by John Davies
(Archive Report Section 4.2)

A total of seventy-eight coins was recovered from the Snettisham Bypass excavation. Fifty-six Roman issues comprise the largest component. There are seventeen post-Roman types and two items are completely illegible (Table 1).

All of the coins recovered are very worn and their full identification has been impaired in a number of cases where no surface detail remained. However, it has been possible to identify the majority of issues from their distinctive shapes and sizes, in combination with other diagnostic features such as portrait silhouettes and isolated lettering.

Plate XI Iron Age coins: Icenian gold stater; silver unit of Pattern-Horse type; gold quarter-stater. Scale 1:1

Issue	Period	Total	Total (Site 1555)
I	to AD41	2	(1)
IIa	41–54		
IIb	54-68	5	(5)
III	69–96	7	(4)
IV	96–117	8	(6)
V	117–138	5	(2)
VI	138–161	6	(1)
VIIa	161–180	4	(3)
VIIb	180–192		
VIII	193–222	1	
IXa	222–238		
IXb	238–259		
X	259–275	2	(1)
XI	275–296	1	
Total		41	(23)
first–second century		12	(10)
third–fourth century		3	(2)
Total Roman		56	(35)
Iron Age		3	(3)
thirteenth–fifteenth century		5	(2)
seventeenth century		12	(3)
illegible		2	(1)
Coin total		78	(44)

Table 1 Chronological breakdown of the coins from Snettisham Bypass, (Site 1555 totals in brackets)

Roman Issues
The bulk of the Roman coins are early in date, with forty-nine of the fifty-six belonging to the first and second centuries, and before. It is unusual for a collection of site finds predominantly to comprise the earlier coins of the

	Denarii		Sestertii		Dupondii		Asses	
Republic	2	*(1)*						
Claudius (irreg.)							2	*(2)*
Nero			1	*(1)*				
Vespasian					1	*(1)*	5	*(2)*
Domitian					1	*(1)*		
Trajan	1	*(1)*	2	*(1)*	3	*(3)*	2	*(1)*
Hadrian			2	*(1)*			3	*(1)*
Antoninus Pius	1		2		1	*(1)*	2	
Marcus Aurelius/ Lucius Verus			2	*(1)*	1	*(1)*	1	*(1)*
Illegible first-second			4	*(3)*	1	*(1)*	6	*(6)*
Total	4	*(2)*	13	*(7)*	7	*(7)*	24	*(14)*

Table 2 Breakdown of first and second-century coin denominations (Site 1555 totals in brackets)

Augustan system and these Snettisham coins are numerous enough to allow some numerical analysis.

The denominations of the Snettisham first and second century issues are recorded in Table 2. Half of the forty-eight recognisable types are *asses*, with *sestertii* accounting for approximately one quarter and *dupondii* much less common. The comparative rarity of *denarii*, with just four examples before AD200, is not surprising, as silver coins are always much rarer among site finds.

The Snettisham Roman coin list opens with two Republican *denarii* and two irregular Claudian *asses*. These particular types comprised much of the coinage used during the immediate post-conquest period and, as such, their presence can often be associated with the site of a military camp, fort or early town. They are found in quantity at the *coloniae*. Coin supply to Britain was not initially a regular process and following the initial input of Claudian *aes* during the conquest period, the years between AD52 and the end of Domitian's reign (AD96) saw only sporadic injection of *aes* denominations into the province (Walker 1988). There were just four but massive injections of *aes* during these years, three of which correspond to recognised periods of activity at the mint of Lugdunum. All of the remaining closely datable coins of the first century from Snettisham fall into the first of these periods, between 64–67, under Nero, and all belong to the mint of Lugdunum.

After AD96 these was a change in the supply of coin to Britain, with the mint of Rome producing a regular supply of *aes*. Coin then entered Britain on a more regular basis and there was a heavier emphasis on the production of *sestertii* while *asses* became less numerous. These changes are detectable among the Snettisham coins, among which Rome is the only mint represented from the reign of Trajan (from AD98) until the arrival of the *antoniniani* of the Gallic Empire, in the late third century. Table 2 also clearly shows the change of emphasis towards the production and supply of *sestertii* from the reign of Trajan onwards.

There is a striking absence of late Roman issues which generally dominate on Roman sites in Britain. The main chronological group from Snettisham ends at the start of the third century with a single *denarius* of Caracalla, struck in AD207. Subsequent issues include just three *antoniniani*, of AD268–84, and no coin can definitely be assigned to the fourth century.

Post-Roman Coinage

There is a gap in the coin list after the late third century until the post-Roman issues begin in the thirteenth century, with a cut halfpenny of King John and a slightly later silver 'long cross' penny of Henry III. Other types of interest include three medieval jetons. The earliest of these was produced in the Low Countries in the fourteenth century; the other two are Nuremberg jetons, which are commonly found in Britain and date from the fifteenth and sixteenth centuries. The remaining post-Roman coins are all halfpennies and farthings dating from Charles II onwards.

III. Copper Alloy Brooches
by D. Mackreth
(Archive Report Section 4.3)

A total of forty-one complete or fragmentary brooches were studied by D.F. Mackreth; the full descriptive catalogue is included in the archive report. The majority of the brooches were recovered by metal detector during the initial topsoil stripping and were unstratified: the stratified groups have been identified in the main body of the text.

All brooches were made from alloys of copper. The majority (21) were classified as Colchester Derivatives, though one 'true' Colchester type was also found (archive catalogue No. 1). This latter brooch has a distinctive design and would appear to have been manufactured somewhere in Norfolk or the southern Fens; although no examples of this design have been dated, the style may indicate the date is late in Colchester's *floruit*: possibly *c.* AD25–50/55.

The Colchester Derivatives are further classified according to the means originally used to secure the spring and pin to the brooch. Ten used a rearward-facing hook, which is a style believed to be typically Icenian on the basis of its dating (*c.* AD40–60/65) and northern East Anglian distribution. (Mackreth 1996). Two are of the 'Harlow' type which are seen as being the successor of the Colchester type in southern East Anglia, and have a *floruit* of *c.* AD40–75/80; and one damaged brooch may have been of the 'Polden Hill' type. Three hybrids of these fixing-styles were identified: hybrids appear to have been very uncommon and the three from the excavation at Snettisham cannot be easily sourced or dated, though it is unlikely that they date to after *c.* AD80. A further four brooches had hinged pins, three also having moulded decoration — a combination which is very unusual and apparently restricted to East Anglia and the eastern Midlands. The distribution and style suggest that this group too is probably earlier than AD60/65, and certainly no later than *c.* AD75.

The other identified brooches consisted of four early post-Conquest Hod Hill types, two penannulars, two late La Tene types, and a Headstud type. All these types appear to have gone out of circulation before the end of the first century AD; no brooches were found which could be dated with certainty to the second century or later.

House 2 and Enclosure (Phase 2)
(Figure 30)

Colchester Derivatives
14. The spring is held by three rearward-facing hooks, one in the middle and one at the end of each wing. The hook has a buried ridge down the middle. The wings and bow are plain. (*41 (First phase of enclosure ditch fill).* SF 43)

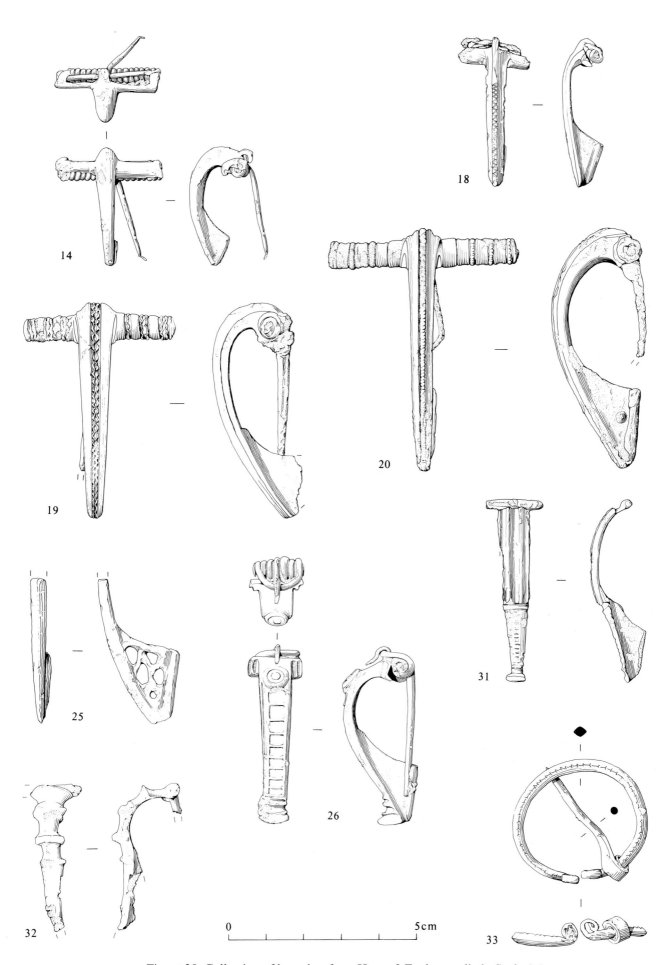

Figure 30 Collection of brooches from House 2 Enclosure ditch. Scale 1:1

53

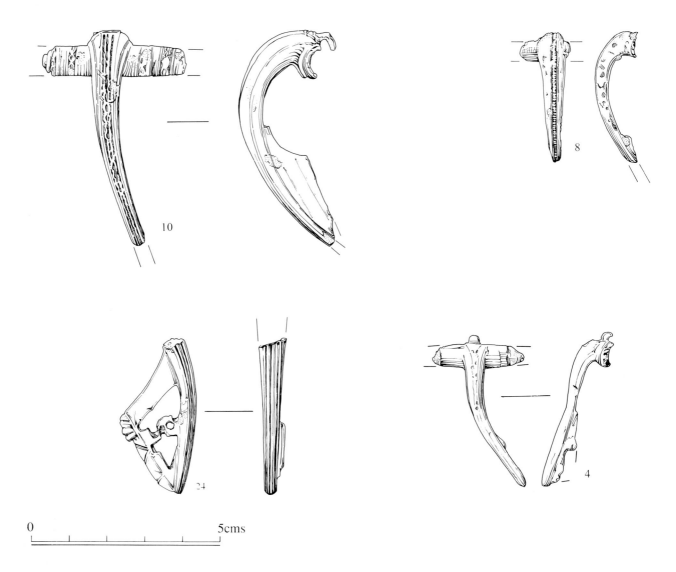

0   5cms

Figure 31 Brooch assemblage, Site 1515. Scale 1:1

18. The spring is held to the body of the brooch by an axis bar passing through the coils of the spring and the lower of two holes in a plate behind the head of the bow; the upper hole holds the chord. Each wing is plain. The plate behind the head of the bow is carried over that to form a skeuomorph of the hook on the Colchester type. The bow has a flat back and squared sides. The front has a concave face on each side and line of rocker-arm ornament down the flat centre. The catch plate is solid. (*187 (First phase enclosure ditch fill).*)

A virtually identical brooch, but with a pierced catchplate was recovered during topsoil removal in the southern part of the excavation area (No. 17, not illustrated).

19. There may be seams across the back of the wings which would show that the axis bar had been inserted after casting. Each wing has a single wavy line ridge next to the bow formed by punching. Between that and the end of the wing are two pairs of opposed wavy lines. The bow has a flat back, squared corners and a step down each side of the front. The centre of that is rounded and has a pair of opposed wavy ridges sunk down the middle. (*22 (Second phase of ditch fill). SF35*)

20. There is a seam across the back of the wings showing that the axis bar was inserted after casting. Each wing has three beaded ridges alternating with pairs of ridges joined by flutes. The bow has the same section as 19. above, only with a beaded ridge down the middle. (*41 (First phase of enclosure ditch fill). SF29*)

Hod Hill Types

31. The upper bow has four equally spaced ridges, separated by flutes, the middle ones being beaded. The lower bow has a flute and a moulding at the top and a line of cross-cuts down the middle to the usual two-part foot-knob. (*187 (First phase of enclosure ditch fill). SF47*)

32. The upper bow has a flaring moulding above three thinner ones each separated by straight sections with chamfered sides. The lower bow has a rounded front. The foot-knob is missing. The tinning or silvering was applied differentially leaving a section with the three thin mouldings plain. (*41 (First phase of enclosure ditch fill). SF31*)

Headstud

26. The axis bar of the spring passes through a pierced lug behind the head of the bow, the chord is held by a forward-facing hook. Each wing has two mouldings, one wide and the other narrow. The circular stud has an annular groove. Each border below the stud has a groove and there are nine rectangular cells down the middle. The enamel has completely decayed, but its condition suggests that there had been two alternating colours. At the base of the bow are cross-mouldings separated from the two-part foot-knob by a flute. (*22 (Second phase of enclosure ditch fill). SF27*)

Penannular

33. The ring has a lozenge section and cross-cuts along the top corner. Each terminal was hammered out and then coiled at right angle to the plane of the ring. The pin has a slight hump. (*41 (First phase of enclosure ditch fill). SF31*)

Unclassified

25. The head is missing. The plain bow is thin and has a rounded front. The catchplate has five piercings arranged as a crude type of fretting. Although the head, with its diagnostic characteristics, is missing the elaborately decorated catchplate appears to be a

deliberate attempt to copy the style of elaborate fretting found on some Colchesters (*e.g.* Stead and Rigby 1989, fig.125,9,11). This would imply that there were still examples to be seen in use and would make the date of manufacture to before 55/60 at the latest. (*167 (Fill of house ditch, northeast sector).* 167)

Rubbish pit group (Phase 2)

Colchester type
n.ill. (No.1) Only the stubs of the spring and hook survive. The remaining wing is very short and plain. The bow is wide and has a slight taper towards the foot, now missing. Down the centre of the bow are two ridges distorted by punching to form opposed wavy lines. (*357 (Fill of Pit 420).* SF 54)

Colchester Derivatives
n.ill. (No. 5) Very corroded, the front face of the wings is hidden. The bow has a flat back, a step down each side and a beaded ridge down the centre of the swelled front. (*357 (Fill of Pit 420).* SF 53)
n.ill. (No.15) The spring is held by three rearward-facing hooks. The hooks are carried down to form ridges, the central one being short, the others running to the bottom of the wings and having another ridge on the inner side. The bow has a ridge between it and each wing, the bow itself is plain and the lower part is missing. (*357 (Fill of Pit 420).* SF 55)

Site 1515
(Figure 31)

Colchester Derivatives
4.   Each wing has two sunken ridges, separated by a flute, at the end. The rest of the brooch is plain. (*23, Fill of Pit 22*)
8.   The surviving parts of the wings are plain. The bow has a flat back and a rounded front down which runs a sunken beaded ridge. (*23, fill of Pit 22*)
10. The complete wing has two pairs of sunken ridges divided by a flute between three sets of two opposed wavy line formed by distorting a pair of buried ridges by punching. The hook is broad with two buried ridges forming a pair of opposed Cs on top. At the foot of the hook is a simplified set of mouldings copying those on the wings. The bow has a flat back, chamfered rear corners, a step down each side and two sunken wavy ridges, formed like those on the wings, down the rounded front. (*23, fill of Pit 22*)

Unclassified
24. Is missing its head; the bow has a lozenge section with two pairs of ridges down the middle. The catchplate has two large piercings which are fretted next to the elaborately-shaped dividing bar which is pierced by a small circle. The start of the return has a vertical groove, and the return itself has a relief 'lip' at the top and, below that, a chevron made up of pairs of grooves. Although the head is missing the elaborately decorated catchplate should be no later than *c*. 75AD. (*23, fill of Pit 22*)

IV. Metalworking Debris

Slag
by Gerry McDonnell
(Archive Report Section 4.4)

Slag Classification
The slag recovered from the excavation of Site 1555 and from Watching Brief sites amounted to 34.8kg in total. The material was visually examined and classified solely on the basis of its morphology into two broad groups: diagnostic slags (*i.e.* those which can be attributed to a particular industrial process) and non-diagnostic, which could have been produced by a variety of processes.

Diagnostic Ferrous Slags and Residues

Smelting Tap Slag
Tap slag is one of the most characteristic forms and is distinguished by the rope-like morphology of the upper cooling surface. The tap slag from Site 1555 was typical and the majority was readily distinguished from the smithing slags. A total of 27.6kg was recorded. The slag ranged in size from fragments < 50mm maximum to larger pieces < 100mm maximum. A few very large lumps weighing in excess of 200g were recovered. Examples of 'slag feeders' (runs of slag that solidified in the furnace tap hole) were recovered from the Phase 5 backfill of Well 1.

Furnace Slag
This smelting slag is characterised by its viscous appearance, and the presence of large charcoal impressions (approximately 25mm in square section and at least 30mm long). There were only a few examples of this slag type from cleaning to the north of Well 1, and the material has not been recorded separately in the archive catalogue (Archive Report Section 4.4).

Smithing Slag
This classification was used for all slag not readily identifiable as smelting by-product; in excess of 2.4kg of this type of slag was noted.

Hearth Bottoms
A plano-convex accumulation of iron silicate forming in the smelting hearth. Only one example was present, coming from Pit *738,* part of the Phase 3 iron processing concentration discovered during the Watching Brief at the north end of Site 1555.

Non-Diagnostic Slags and Residues

Hearth Lining
The clay lining of an industrial hearth/furnace/kiln with a vitrified or slag-attacked face. It is often impossible to distinguish between furnace and hearth lining. A total of 3.7kg of this material was recovered from the 1989 fieldwork, with a sub-rectangular furnace lining fragment being found in the third/fourth-century backfill of Well 1. This has been described more fully above in Chapter 4.

Cinder
High silica-content slag, which can form either at the reaction zone between the smithing slag and the hearth lining, or by high temperature reaction between silica and ferruginous material. Only 67g of this class of slag was recovered.

Other Residues
This class comprised possible ore fragments, ferruginous concretion (probably naturally formed), and fragments of fired clay. 1.0kg of this material was recorded.

Distribution of the Slag
The slag recovered during detailed excavation, fieldwalking, and in the Watching Brief has been catalogued in the Archive Report (Section 4.4). Slag was recorded in a total of seventy-five contexts along the whole length of the excavation; only a few contained a weight of slag greater than 1kg (a figure taken to represent potentially significant deposits). The greatest quantities of tap slag were recovered from the unstratified layers, with appreciable stratified quantities coming only from the backfill of Well 1. The distribution of the hearth/furnace lining reflected that of the smelting slag and it is therefore

probable that the lining is furnace lining, which would indicate that the smelting area was close to the part of Site 1555 excavated in 1989. The quantities of smithing slag, cinder and other material are background levels only.

Discussion

The distribution of the slag in excavated features showed no concentrations pointing to areas of smelting activity. The occurrence of large deposits in the plough soil on Site 1555 and in large features suggests that the slag has spread from an ironworking area close to the excavation.

The slag is typical tap smelting slag, which is common in the Roman period, although the presence of a piece of probable furnace lining which was only slightly curved does suggest the presence of furnace types other than the most common shaft furnaces of the 'Ashwicken' type (Tylecote and Owles 1960).

Conclusions

The evidence recovered from excavation and fieldwalking indicates that there was Roman iron smelting close to the line of the present day Snettisham bypass. It is possible that the activity could be earlier, and the slag occurring in the Roman contexts is residual. The scale of the activity cannot be determined, *i.e.* there is insufficient evidence to suggest whether there were just a few smelting operations to satisfy an immediate need or there was a minor industrial activity. The slag is typical iron smelting tap slag with some furnace slag present.

Moulds and Crucibles

by C. Mortimer

(Archive Report Section 4.5)

Approximately eighty small sherds recovered from the Phase 1 industrial waste pit *730* were examined. The material consisted of various forms in various degrees of oxidation, and was categorised as crucible or mould fragments on the basis of form and degree of oxidation.

Many of the pieces whose surfaces are predominantly reduced-fired are thought to be crucible fragments. On the whole they are too small for their original forms to be reconstructed, or their diameters estimated. The cross-sections are rather irregular so they were probably hand built. They may have been dish- or bowl-shaped with rims pinched out to form pouring lips. Most crucibles found in the 1989 excavations are thick (up to 12mm) and their fabrics have a somewhat coarser texture than the moulds, sometimes with large inclusions. The forms discovered at this site are consistent with late Iron Age forms (Spratling *et al.* 1980, fig. 2).

Vitrification is evident at the edge of several pieces, either on the inside or on both the inside and outside of the fragments. This may suggest that heating was from above. A selection of these areas was tested using qualitative non-destructive x-ray fluorescence (XRF), as were a smaller number of metal-rich deposits and some inside surfaces with unusual colouring. A representative group of results is recorded below in the Metalworking Debris Summary, and in the Archive Report (Section 4.5). The XRF results suggest that copper alloys containing zinc, lead and tin were being melted at this site, though the exact alloy(s) involved cannot be determined.

Mould fragments are identified by the presence of object impressions (the area of the impression normally being strongly reduced by contact with the hot metal), and

by a relatively fine-textured and clean fabric. Frequently the outsides of moulds are oxidised through being in contact with air whilst at elevated temperatures (*i.e.* during pre-heating and casting). However a number of moulds from the excavation had thinner sections or were exposed to the reducing atmosphere for longer so that their fabrics were reduced throughout.

Identifiable Forms

(Figure 32)

Although fragments are generally small, some can be identified as parts of piece moulds.

1. Mould fragment apparently for a ring, 60–70mm in diameter, with rounded elements projecting from it. It is suggested that the mould would be suitable for casting terrets. Pieces from the upper and lower valves of this mould can be distinguished by the nature of the outer rim of the mould; these areas may be either concave or convex and would have fitted together to make a smooth join. When fitted together the mould appears to have been doughnut-shaped externally (*i.e.* annular with a very small central hole).

2. Several pieces of a tapering cylinder with minimum internal diameter of slightly less than 20mm, flaring out to a diameter of at least 40mm. Although this is the type of profile expected for a sprue cup, the diameter is too large. It is difficult to know which end was uppermost in casting; at the wider end the smoothed outside surfaces of the mould are consistently broken off, a feature which may relate to some sort of luting which joined this part of the mould to another part, causing the surface to be pulled away when the mould was taken apart. At the other end of several of the pieces there is a slight ridge which would suggest a mould form with a broad rounded bulge, about 5mm wide. This ridge is also visible on other pieces in the assemblage. If these pieces are indeed associated, the form evidently continued into a curving shape, with a much sharper curvature than the flared piece discussed above. A possible reconstruction has been suggested (Figure 32.2). With this size of object, it is likely that the casting would have been hollow and thus required an inner ceramic core. Some pieces with this detail are oxidised and others reduced on the surface, suggesting that they are not all from the same casting operation, and therefore that this form may have been made more than once at this site.

3. Mould fragment with a flat base and an almost square corner. Inside the base there seems to be a slight upturn. This piece could be from a bar ingot mould, in which case this upturn may be the lower part of an outside wall. An ingot mould is quite likely, as this piece appears to be from an open mould.

Subsequent to the metalworking debris analysis four fragments of possibly three additional moulds were identified during study of the fired clay from the 'cleaning' context in the same area.

4. Mould fragment consisting of a concave terminal banded by a ridge, with an apparently curving shank extending beyond the edge of the fragment. The edge surface of the mould, if any, has been lost, as has the continuation to the shank.

5, 6. Fragments of mould for an essentially flat object, with a smooth everted surface. The edges of the mould appear to have been broken off, leaving no traces on the fragments in Figure 32.6. Figure 32.5 shows part of an object with a tapering longitudinal ridge; the two fragments in Figure 32.6 appear to be two related parts, possibly of the same object as Figure 32.5 on the basis of their shape.

A selection of vitrified mould and crucible fragments, and a smaller number of metal-rich and anomalously coloured fragments were subjected to qualitative non-destructive x-ray fluorescence to determine the constituent metals (Table 3). The vitreous areas gave little indication of non-ferrous metal types, but the metallic areas and inside surfaces were more illuminating. The XRF results suggest that copper alloys containing zinc and lead were being melted at this site. (A more complete discussion of the results is provided in the Archive Report Section 4.5).

In conclusion we can say that copper alloys containing zinc, tin and lead were melted and cast on the site, producing a number of artefact types. It is likely that the crucible and mould fragments came from the same metalworking system.

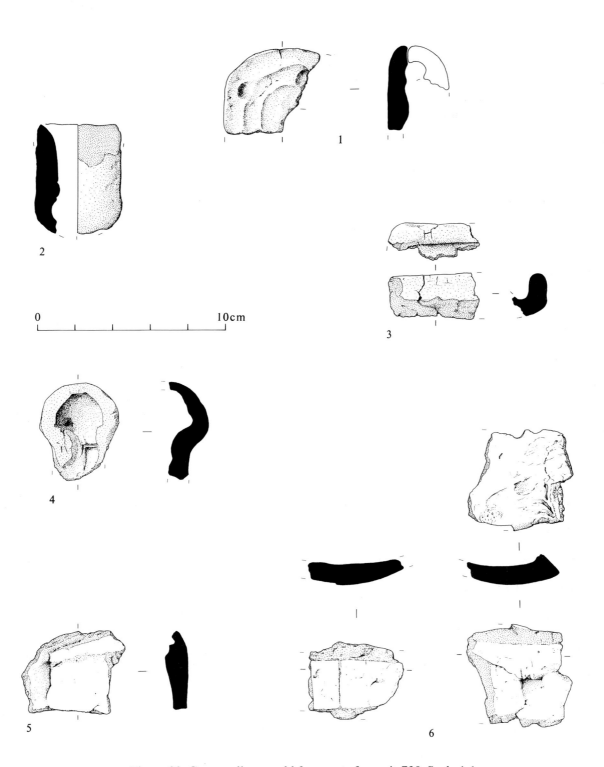

Figure 32 Copper alloy mould fragments from pit *730*. Scale 1:1

XRF Analysis of surfaces: Crucibles

Context	Area	Results
665	Metallic lump	Pb Cu Zn
730	Large frag, metal blobs	Cu Zn Pb Sn
	Slag, red and green	Cu Sn Pb
	Pouring lip – orange	Cu Pb
	Slag	Zn Pb Cu Sn
	Inside a pouring lip	Zn Pb

XRF Analysis of surfaces: Moulds

Context	Area	Results
730	?terret (inside)	Zn Pb
"	terret	Zn Pb (Cu)
"	?fitting	Pb Zn (Cu)
"	corner 'ingot' piece	Cu Pb

Note: Elements are listed approximately in order of peak heights in XRF spectra. Those in brackets are present in very low quantities.

Table 3 XRF analysis of moulds and crucibles

V. Glass

by J. Price and S. Cottam
(Archive Report Section 4.6)

The excavations at Snettisham produced thirty-nine fragments from seven vessels. Thirty-three of these were colourless, and six blue/green. Heavy iridescence was present on the group of fragments making up a cylindrical bottle (No. 2 in Archive Report and Figure 33), but the remaining fragments, particularly those of blue/green glass, showed little weathering.

The seven vessels represented comprised a colourless cup or beaker (No. 1), a cylindrical bottle (No. 2), two possible flask or unguent bottles (Nos 3, 4), one cylindrical and one prismatic blue/green bottles (Nos 5, 6), and an unidentifible sherd (No. 7). The cup and clear bottle both appear to be of types current in the second century, though the bottle is similar to types manufactured from the second to the fourth centuries.

Illustrated Glass Vessels
(Figure 33)

1. Thirteen body fragments, many joining, probably from a beaker. Colourless. Straight side tapering in to constriction, then expanding out. Part of two indents on side below constriction. Horizontal marvered trail at constriction. Small bubbles. Found in the late third-century backfill (*634*) of Well 1. Fragments from the rim and base of a similar indented cup, with horizontal trail below the rim, were found in a second-century context in the drain deposit of the Commandant's House at Housesteads (Charlesworth 1971, 34, no. 6).

2. Twenty fragments, shoulder, body and base, cylindrical bottle. Pale green/colourless. Slight constriction on body below shoulder. Concave base. Two horizontal abraded bands on upper body. At least two further bands on body. Vertical scratch marks. Ring of wear on base edge. Patchy, flaking iridescence. Some fragments pitted. Recovered from a complex of rubbish pits (*128*) close to Well 1. Colourless vessels with cylindrical bodies occur at various times from the second to the fourth centuries. For instance, similar though smaller vessels with either two 'dolphin' handles or no handles, or no neck and a hole-mouth with a tubular edge, are known from York (Harden 1962, 140, fig. 90 H.G.146.1–4 and 141 fig. 89 H.G.182). The shape of the shoulder fragment indicates that the Snettisham bottle had a neck, and it is likely that these fragments come from a large bottle with one angular handle, although no evidence for a handle now survives.

Two of the best examples of this type come from Hauxton, Cambridgeshire (Harden 1958, 13 fig. 6) and Corbridge (Charlesworth 1959, 54 fig. 10 no. 1). Fragments from similar vessels have been found at Caerwent (Boon 1974, 112 no. 3a–c fig. 1), Chew Valley Lake (Harden 1977, 289, nos 21 and 22) and other sites in Britain.

These bottles were probably free-blown, being marvered to form the cylindrical body. The presence of decoration on some examples suggests that these vessels were intended as tableware rather than as household containers, although it has been suggested that the abraded bands might indicate liquid measurements (Boon 1974, 112 no. 3a–c).

3. Two rim and neck fragments, jug or flask. Blue/green. Irregular rim, bent out, up and in. Cylindrical neck. Heat damaged. Recovered from the rubbish pits (*128*) close to Well 1. The fragments probably come from a flask, unguent bottle or jug (for example Isings 1957, Forms 16, 28b, 52 and 55). Jugs in blue/green or strongly coloured glass are common in the north-western provinces in the first and second centuries.

The other four vessels represented are less complete and have not been illustrated.

4. One fragment from the lower body of a tubular unguent bottle (Isings 1957, Form 8). This type of unguent bottle is a frequent find on first century sites in most Roman provinces. The complete vessel

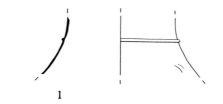

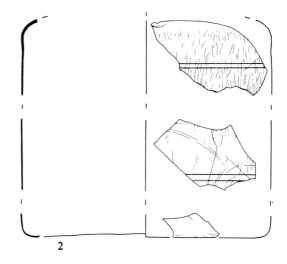

Figure 33 Glass vessels, Site 1555. Scale 1:1

would have had an out-turned rim with a sheared edge, a long narrow neck with a tooled constriction between neck and body, a gently expanding body and a convex base. Production of this form seems to have ended in the early Flavian period.

5, 6. Both these fragments come from blue/green bottles which were produced for the containment of liquid and semi-liquid substances and were in common use throughout the Roman world during the first and second centuries. No. 5 comes from a cylindrical bottle (Isings 1957, Form 51) found in a Phase 3 ditch fill, and No. 6 from a prismatic bottle from Phase 2.

Cylindrical bottles were widely used during the first century, especially from the Flavian period onward, and seem to have gone out of production in the early second century.

Prismatic bottles area also found on first-century sites, but are more long-lived. The form of the rim, neck and handle are identical to those of cylindrical bottles. Prismatic bottles however are nearly always mould-blown, with a variety of base designs. The most common form, the square bottle (Isings 1957, Form 50), continues in use throughout the second century. Signs of scratching where the bottle has been lifted in and out of a case are often visible on these containers, and can be seen on one of the prismatic body fragments from this site (No. 6).

7. This fragment curves slightly in two directions, but is too small for identification to be possible.

VI. Samian

by B. Dickinson
(Archive Report Section 4.7)

Since much of this collection of samian is unstratified and some of it is badly eroded, no attempt has been made to quantify it. It is clear, however, that this is a typical assemblage for a British site occupied continuously from the first century to the end of the second century, or beyond. A full descriptive catalogue has been included in the Archive Report (Section 4.7). Important individual groups are described below.

The ready availability of samian from La Graufesenque and Lezoux is reflected here, the largest quantities of discarded material falling in the Flavian and Antonine periods. It is just possible that the site was first occupied in pre-Flavian times. A stamped dish of Primus from the Phase 1 industrial waste pit *750* (described in Chapter 4, II) and a few of the decorated bowls can scarcely be later than AD 65, but it is more likely that the foundation date fell in the early 70s. Two bowls of Form 37 in the style of Germanus have footrings approximating to those on Form 29 and one of them is clearly stylistically early; the Form 30 vessels and the stamped bowl of Crucuro are also early Flavian. Many of the Form 18 dishes almost certainly belong to the 70s.

The scarcity of vessels from Les Martres-de-Veyre is almost certainly more a matter of availability than an indication of reduced occupation in the Trajanic period.

The range of Hadrianic and early Antonine Lezoux plain ware includes many examples of Forms 18/31 and 18/31R, a few of Form 27 and single vessels of Forms 81 and Curle 11, but these are outnumbered by the mid and late Antonine forms, some of which, like Forms 31R, 79, 80 and a gritted mortarium, will be later than AD 160. There are also two cups of Form 40, uncommon in Central Gaul, which are likely to belong to the late second century. The Hadrianic and early Antonine decorated ware includes bowls by the Sacer i group (3), Pugnus ii or Mapillus, X–5 and the Cerialis ii- Cinnamus ii group. Most of the later decorated ware, with the possible exception of Form 30 in Cinnamus's developed style, is after AD 160.

It is likely that some of the East Gaulish material is early third-century, though there is no certain evidence that any of it is later than the latest second-century Lezoux ware from the excavation. It is nearly all from Rheinzabern, but at least one vessel is from the Argonne, two are from the mainly Hadrianic-Antonine factory of La Madeleine and there is a single example from Trier. The amount of East Gaulish samian is not unremarkable for eastern Britain in general, but is small compared with some other East Anglian sites, such as Burgh-by-Woodbridge (Dickinson and Hartley 1988, 30), Brancaster (Dickinson and Bird 1985, 82), Caister-on-Sea (Dickinson 1993) and West Stow (Hartley and Dickinson 1990, 91), where samian seems to have continued in use until it ceased to be imported into Britain c. AD 260. The samian from this excavation suggests some activity in the first part of the third century, perhaps followed by a break in occupation.

Illustrated Samian
(Figure 34)

House 2 Assemblage (Phase 2)
1. *Form 37*, drilled for mending. Dating to c. AD70–95. Joining sherds were found in the north-west part of the House ring-ditch and the south-west part of the enclosure ditch. A wide panel contains two dogs, a stag, a hare(?) and a curious seven-beaded rosette, which looks more Central than South Gaulish. The adjacent panel has a corner tassel with a cordate bud. The trident-tongued ovolo was used at La Graufesenque by Memor, Mommo and a potter whose name begins with Prim-. The bowl cannot be assigned with certainty to any of these three, but Prim- has a very similar, if not identical, chevron wreath on signed bowls from Caerleon (forthcoming) and Richborough. Memor has the stag on a bowl from Rottweil (Knorr 1909, taf. IV, 1). (*41, Enclosure ditch backfill*)
2. *Form 29*, South Gaulish. The scroll in the upper zone includes a trilobed bud, of a type used at La Graufesenque in the pre-Flavian period. It is very like one noted on bowls stamped by Ingenuus ii (Knorr 1919, taf. 42, 48) and dates to c. AD45–65. (*40, dog burial backfill*)

Phase 4
3. *Form 30*, South Gaulish, with ovolo similar to sherds found in the backfill of the Phase 2 house enclosure. It occurs, together with the hollow rosette junction-masks, on two signed bowls of Memor in the Pompeii Hoard (Atkinson 1914, nos 73–74). The Cupid is a variant of 0.393. *Archive reference: 531ii. (531, Fill of Enclosure 7 ditch 588)*
4. Half a *Form 37* South Gaulish bowl made up of four joining fragments. This vessel has a footring like that on Form 29, but without the groove underneath. The decoration is typical of Germanus i's early style, and has four-pronged ovolo (Knorr 1919, taf. 35, 80) and three straight wreaths over a zone of festoons. The trifid wreath and the festoons and spirals are on form 29 from Trier and the bifid wreath is on another from Nijmegen (Knorr 1919, taf. 37G). Both these have internal stamps of Germanus and are dated to c. AD65/70–85. *Archive reference: 531iii. (531, Fill of Enclosure 7 ditch 588)*

Well 1 Assemblage (Phase 5)
5. The vessel is about three-quarters complete and approximates to Ludowici's Tf, but has no barbotine above the flange. It was never stamped. Late second or early third century. (*678*)
6. *Form 37*, Central Gaulish, with ovolo Rogers B184 and a border of flat, rectangular beads. The bear (0.1589) was used at Lezoux by Paternus v, but there is no other connection with him. Certainly Antonine and probably after AD160.

VII. Mortaria

by David Gurney
(Archive Report Section 4.8)

The mortaria examined derive from three components of the 1989 fieldwork, namely the subsoil features, unstratified in the ploughsoil and from the Watching Brief. The sample as a whole is small, perhaps representing thirty-seven vessels (ten from stratified contexts, sixteen from unstratified, eleven from Watching Brief). Vessels have been individually described in the Archive Report (Section 4.8). Most drawable rims have been illustrated.

The majority of the mortaria probably come from small local East Anglian (Norfolk) workshops, and there are relatively few traded vessels. There is a single sherd from Brockley Hill (No. 1), and the Nene Valley accounts for only two vessels (Nos 10, 19), both in the standard fabric; this, combined with the absence of Oxford/Hadham mortaria may suggest that the later Roman occupation was not intensive, assuming that the sample is representative. One may also note the absence of reduced (grey) mortaria, which are now being recognised as an important feature of later third- and fourth-century assemblages in the county, as, for example, on the east coast at Caister-on-Sea.

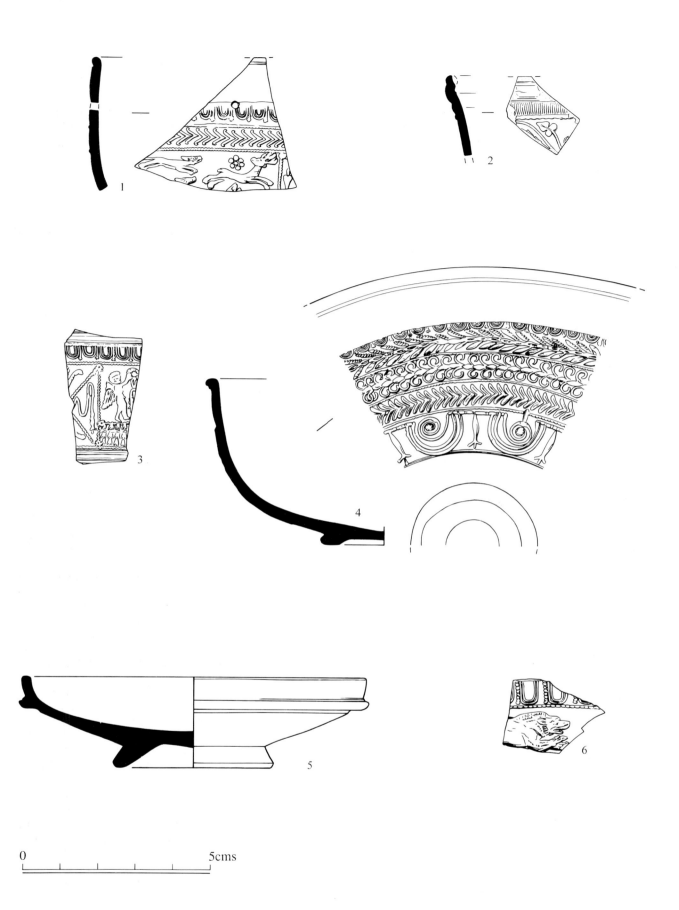

Figure 34 Illustrated samian. Scale 1:1

Also apparently unrepresented are mortaria from the Nar Valley (Pentney, Shouldham area), reeded-rim types in oxidised fabrics with black iron ore trituration grit showing a strong Nene Valley influence and perhaps an offshoot of that industry. The fabrics of three of the mortaria (Nos 12–14) are not dissimilar to Nar Valley vessels and could be the products of a West Norfolk workshop, but they appear to have trituration of quartz and flint rather than the usual black iron ore.

Two vessels call for special comment, and these are the two stamped mortaria (Figure 35). Mrs Kay Hartley has kindly provided details of these. The first (No. 1) is from the fill of the enclosure ditch associated with House 2 in Phase 2 of the site, and has a stamp of Secundus, who appears to have been producing vessels from Brockley Hill in the mid-late first century. The second stamp (No. 33) from Site 1515 north of the Ingol is likely to have been intended as 'Crescens', who seems to have been working around Baylham, near Ipswich, again in the mid-late first century.

It would appear that most of the mortaria are of probable East Anglian origin, with relatively few traded vessels. The Norfolk market for mortaria in the third and fourth centuries was largely supplied by the potteries of the lower Nene Valley, but only two vessels from this source are represented. Most of the mortaria are probably of second-century date, a period when mortaria were produced at many local workshops in Norfolk, supplying only local communities. The potteries at Brampton and Ellingham were of greater regional importance, but their products do not appear to be represented here. While it is probable that most of the mortaria were produced in Norfolk, the presence of vessels from other parts of East Anglia, like that from Baylham near Ipswich is also likely. The mortaria suggest occupation mainly in the first and second centuries, with only slight activity in the third and fourth centuries.

Illustrated vessels
(Figure 35)
1. Hard granular greyish-cream fabric; pink core; abundant well-sorted quartz with sparse red inclusions; tituration grit flint and quartz. The vessel is stamped from a die which gives SECVNVSF. Brockley Hill *c.* AD60–90 (Inf Mrs K. Hartley). Three sherds *22*, one joining *41 (All from House 2's Enclosure backfills)*
2. Very hard fine fabric; pinkish core, creamy margins, yellowish slipped surface; sparse quartz inclusions. Trituration grit moderate generally fine white quartz. ?3rd century. (*128, unstratified concentration*)
4. Hard fine fabric; cream; moderate fine quartz with sparse red inclusions. Trituration grit flint. ?2nd century. (*128, unstratified concentration*).
6. Hard fairly fine fabric; cream core and surface, light red margins; sparse quartz and very sparse red iron ore inclusions; smoothed surface. No trituration grit extant. ?3rd century. (*128, unstratified concentration*)
7. Very hard fine off-white fabric; very sparse quartz and reddish-brown inclusions; smoothed surface. No trituration grit extant. Probably same vessel as No. 24 (not illustrated). ?3rd century. (*128, unstratified concentration*)
12. Hard light red fabric with moderate quartz; lighter reddish yellow surfaces. Quartz and flint trituration grit. ?mid 2nd century. (*106, Topsoil*)
13. Similar fabric to 12, but with creamy pinkish core and light red margins; ?creamy slip. ?2nd century. (*106, Topsoil*)

17. Hard dense slightly greenish fabric, pale brown surfaces; sparse quartz and red and black inclusions. Flint trituration grit. ?2nd century. (*106, Topsoil*)
18. Hard dense light brown fabric with sparse quartz inclusions. Flint and quartz trituration grit. ?2nd century. (*106, Topsoil*); almost-certain body sherd (not illustrated, No. 8) recovered from *521 (unstratified)*
19. Castor-Stibbington area of Lower Nene Valley. 3rd/4th century. (*106, Topsoil*)
23. Fairly hard dense reddish-yellow fabric with paler core; sparse fine quartz inclusions. Flint trituration grit. ?mid-2nd century. (*106, Topsoil*)
26. Soft pinkish fabric with sparse quartz and red and black inclusions. Flint with some quartz trituration grit. (*106, Topsoil*)
29. Fairly soft pinkish fabric; sparse quartz and reddish inclusions. Flint trituration grit. ?2nd century. (*107, Topsoil*)
33. The fabric of this is fine-textured, intended to be darkish-cream, though discoloured due to chemical weathering; sparse quartz and reddish brown and black inclusions, flint and quartz trituration grit. The most obvious reading of the stamp would give Crescuari, but it is more likely that Crescens is intended (E represented by II, S reversed, EN ligatured, S reversed). ?Baylham, Suffolk, AD60–90. (Inf. Mrs K. Hartley) *Site 1515 (18, Fill of Trackway Ditch 16)*

VIII. Amphorae
by D. Williams
(Archive Report Section 4.9)

A small number of amphora fragments were recovered (101 sherds; 10,926g). Many of the fragments came from the initial topsoil removal over the excavation site (forty-three sherds, including the larger fragments), though fragments were found during the Watching Brief and from stratified deposits. A full listing is provided in the Archive Report (Section 4.9).

The most common type identified was Dressel 20, which is the most common form found on Romano-British sites (Williams and Peacock 1983). It was made along the banks of the river Guadalquivir and its tributaries between Seville and Cordoba in the southern Spanish province of Baetica, and used for the long-distance carriage of the local olive oil. With some typological development, mainly to the rims, this globular-shaped amphora type was in production throughout most of the Roman occupation of Britain. Two rims were recovered from Snettisham, and these can be given approximate dates of AD75–150 and mid-second century when compared with the detailed typology of Dressel 20 rims from Augst illustrated by Martin-Kilcher (1983). In addition, two body sherds contain graffiti, one of which may also have a possible letter inscribed in black ink. Sherds of Dressel 20 amphorae were recovered from Sites 1555 and 1515

A number of plain body sherds which probably belong to the flat-bottomed southern French amphorae form Gauloise 4 were recovered. This type was used predominantly to transport wine from this region (Laubenheimer 1985); in Britain, this type first appears shortly after the Boudiccan revolt, following which it becomes very common up to the late third or early fourth centuries AD (Peacock 1978; Peacock and Williams 1986, Class 27). This type was only recorded on Site 1555.

Two handles of a possibly Gallic type and several undesignated types were also recovered from Site 1555 and the Watching Brief areas immediately north and south (Sites 1515 and 20199).

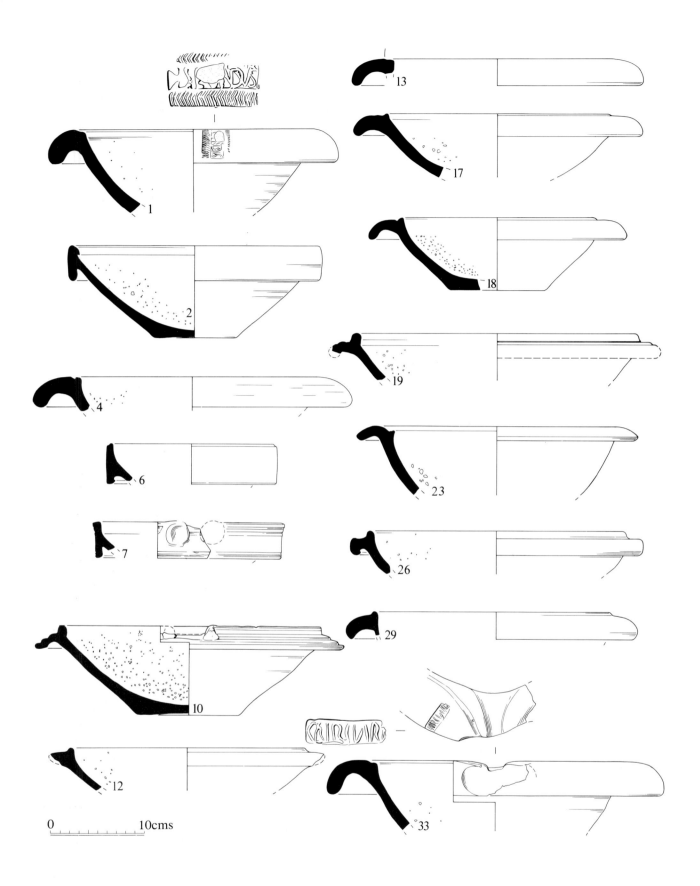

Figure 35 Mortaria assemblage, Sites 1555 and 1515. Scale 1:4

IX. Coarse Pottery

by M. Flitcroft
(Archive Report Section 6)

Introduction

A little over 148kg of pottery was recovered from Site 1555. 70kg of this derived from the topsoil, and this material was rapidly assessed, though no detailed fabric and form quantification was made. A further 27kg was recovered during the Watching Brief, of which 12kg was post-Roman.

The 1989 fieldwork produced the first sizeable assemblage of pottery covering the transition from Iron Age to Romano-British pottery traditions in Norfolk, and as such supplements the Fabric and Form series for later assemblages from Brancaster (Andrews 1985), Caister on Sea (in Darling and Gurney 1993) and Billingford, Norfolk (Lyons forthcoming), whilst providing comparison with the assemblages from broadly contemporary Fenland sites.

This summary will outline the range of material present on the site and characterise the differences between 'early' and 'late' assemblages, as well as discussing the information the coarse pottery can provide on the social and economic life of the early Roman settlement at Snettisham. A catalogue of contexts is included in the Archive Report (Section 6).

The assemblages from the separate groups of contexts were studied individually and compared to establish similarities and to document the changes in the nature of the site over time. Summaries of the assemblages from each phase of the site are given below; this section also attempts to describe the overall composition of the ceramic assemblage and the variations between phases.

A site Fabric and Form series were established as a possible basis for part of a County-wide series, and the fabric descriptions are presented below. The range of fabrics and forms present in each phase are described below and have been summarised in the phase descriptions in Chapter 4. It is considered that the wholesale publishing of the site form series in this section of the report would be of limited value.

Analysis Methodology

Recognisable sherds of samian, amphorae and mortaria were quantified, removed and sent for specialist study. The coarse pottery and remaining finewares were recorded by context using pro-forma catalogue sheets. Initial work on the pottery assemblage was undertaken by Phil Copleston; this quantification was subsequently completed and enhanced by M. Flitcroft. Material from the unstratified topsoil of Site 1555 was not studied intensively, but was scanned and weighed.

Each context was divided into fabrics based on visual inspection of the ceramic matrix; type sherds of each fabric were removed to act as a reference standard. Each fabric was given a code number based on its broad type (Reduced, Oxidised) and the varieties within this type (*e.g.* Grey, White). Fabrics were also given a Common Name, either the source (in the case of material from known industries) or a descriptive name.

The type of each sherd was noted (rim, base, decorated body, plain body, handle...) and assigned to a broad form type whenever possible. Closer definition into specific form types was made for all rim sherds which retained sufficient profile; for other rims the basic shape was recorded in broader categories such as Everted, Flaring, Hooked *etc.*

The ceramic material was quantified by mass and sherd numbers within each sherd-type, fabric and context. All percentage figures quoted are proportions by mass rather than sherd count. Rims and bases were additionally described by measurement of their curvature and percentage of original vessel surviving (the EVE measurement). Due to the small number of sherds in which the specific forms were recognisable, analysis of the form categories was generally conducted on the basis of maximum number of vessels present. For this measure sherds not obviously from the same vessel were counted as separate vessels, which gave the advantage of including the large number of body sherds in the quantification. Decoration was noted, as were any other traces of sooting/wear *etc.*

Pottery from Site 1555 was input onto computer for detailed analysis; the smaller quantity of material from the Watching Brief was not.

Fabrics
(Figure 44, Table 4)

The pottery was divided by broad appearance into four classes: reduced wares, grey wares, oxidised wares and white wares. Classes were further subdivided as necessary to account for the different fabrics present in each.

Reduced Wares

Reduced fabrics (principally wares with reduced firing and black surfaces) account for 47.4% of the total non-ploughsoil pottery assemblage. Of the seven fabrics, only R1, R2/R5 and R4 were found in any real quantities (the remaining three fabrics account for 3.7% of the total non-topsoil assemblage by mass); R4 was by far the most abundant fabric, accounting for 26.3% of the site total by mass. This fabric was most common in the earliest phase, where it formed around three-quarters of the small assemblage, but continues to be a significant element throughout the history of the site.

Fabric R3, although relatively uncommon on the main excavation (Site 1555), was a more frequent find in the assemblage from the salvage excavations on Site 1515.

Reduced Fabric Types

R1   Grey-brown interior surface, orange or black/grey exterior; dark grey-black core. Hard, rough fabric with hackly/laminated fracture containing quantities of medium/coarse quartz grains.

R2   Brown-black surfaces, grey-brown core. A hard rough fabric with fine or hackly fracture containing finer quartz grains than R1. One of the more common fabrics, most common in the middle phases of the site. Waster sherds in this fabric were recovered from Site 1515 (Figure 43, No. 69.)

R3   Grey interior, speckled light and dark exterior surfaces; light grey core with brown margins. A hard smooth fabric containing medium-sized rounded quartz grains and a few coarse red grog fragments.

R4   Black or very dark grey surfaces and core. A hard, rough fabric with a hackly fracture, containing abundant medium/coarse rounded quartz and some very coarse grog fragments. In its handmade forms, this is the diagnostic early fabric; it is the predominant fabric of the early phases of the site. The fabric is broadly similar to that of the Nar valley industries' products, but the form range and dating imply that it is not a product of these kilns and it is probably best described as a product of the local clays.

R5   This fabric is very similar to R2 and has been amalgamated with it.

R6   Dark grey/black surfaces; black core. Hard or very hard smooth micaceous fabric with a fine/hackly fracture containing moderate amounts of quartz and grog.

R7   Dark brown-black surfaces; dark grey-black core. Fairly soft smooth fabric with a hackly fracture containing large quantities of shell, and moderate amounts of quartz.

Grey Wares

The (reduced) grey wares were the second most populous fabric class, accounting for 31% of the stratified and semi-stratified assemblage by mass. Fabrics G2 and G5 were the most common, with significant minor proportions of G1 and G4 (2% and 3% of the site total respectively). Grey ware fabrics, particularly the hard sandy G5, became the predominant coarse ware fabrics in the later phases of the site.

Grey Fabric Types

G1   Dark grey-black surface; grey core. A hard, rough fabric very similar to R1 but containing additional moderate amounts of mica and buff grog.

G2   Mid-grey surfaces; blue-grey core. Very hard, rough sandy fabric with a fine fracture, containing moderate numbers of medium-sized organic voids, and a little mica. This fabric is typical of the later phases of the site. Waster sherds in this fabric were recovered from Site 1515 (Figure 43, No. 68).

G3   Light grey surface and core. This smooth fabric has a hard surface, but softer core with a smooth fracture, and contains large quantities of quartzite and some grog fragments.

G4   Mid-grey surfaces and core. A moderately hard, rough fabric with a fine fracture, containing abundant angular quartz giving a speckled appearance.

G5   Light grey surfaces; core sometimes slightly darker. A very hard sandy fabric with a smooth or fine fracture containing abundant quartz, and moderate amounts of large black grog fragments. Fabrics G4 and G5 are very similar to the products of the Brampton industry, as described by Andrews (1985).

G6   Dark blue-grey surfaces; light grey core. A hard fabric with smoothed or burnished surfaces and a fine fracture containing common quartz fragments. This fabric is very similar to Nene Valley Grey Ware products (as described by Andrews for Brancaster, 1985).

G7   Mid-grey surfaces; dark grey core. A hard, rough sandy fabric with a fine or hackly fracture containing abundant quartz, and a few fragments of flint. This fabric appears similar to that of the Nar Valley industry based around Shouldham and Pentney.

Oxidised Wares

Oxidised wares accounted for 16.2% of the site total, with the more common fabrics (OX1, OX2, OX3) accounting for 67% of the oxidised total (*i.e.* 10.9% of the coarse ware total). OX1 appears to be an 'early' fabric, having its *floruit* in Phase 1, whereas OX2 and OX3, used in a variety of romanised forms, only become significant from Phase 2 onwards (*i.e.* from the end of the first century).

Oxidised Fabric Types

OX1   Black surfaces, red-brown core. Hard rough fabric with hackly fracture containing common ill-sorted quartz grains and a little fine mica.

OX2   Reddish-brown surfaces, greyer core. Hard smooth or soapy fabrics with a hackly fracture. The fabric contains common very coarse organic voids (both rounded and angular), moderate fine mica, and sparse coarse/very coarse rounded grog.

OX3   Light orange surfaces and core. Hard smooth or soapy fabric with a smooth fracture containing moderate quantities of medium/coarse rounded quartz.

OX4   Light buff fabric, occasionally with a greyer core. Hard, smooth matrix containing a sparse quantity of rounded quartz. Overfired kiln waste sherds in this fabric were recovered from Site 1515.

OX5   Dark orange/brown surfaces, brownish core. Soft rough fabric with a hackly fracture containing abundant medium or coarse rounded quartz.

OX6   Light orange surface and core. Hard rough fabric with hackly fracture containing common medium or coarse rounded quartz and a few large rounded organic voids.

OX7   Buff surfaces, buff or yellow core. Hard smooth fabric containing a few rounded quartz grains.

OX8   Buff or brown surfaces, buff or grey core. Very hard, harsh fabric with a smooth fracture. Inclusions of abundant coarse angular or sub-rounded quartz.

OX9   Orange interior, buff exterior surfaces with an orange/grey core. A soft, rough fabric with laminated fracture containing common medium-sized angular quartz, common medium-sized organic voids and sparse very coarse grog.

OX10   Pale orange/red surfaces and core. Very hard smooth fabric with a rough core and fine fracture. Inclusions: common medium-sized rounded quartz, and a sparse medium-sized rounded mineral, possibly garnet.

OX11   Pale pink surfaces and core. Soft soapy fabric with smooth fracture, containing sparse quantities of coarse rounded quartz and medium-sized rounded iron ore particles. The interior is gritted with moderate quantities of coarse sub-angular black mineral. Mortarium fabric.

White Wares

The white wares are never a substantial part of the coarse pottery assemblage, accounting for 4.4% of the site total.

White Fabric Types

W1   Pale buff surfaces, light brown core. Fairly soft soapy fabric with a fine fracture. Inclusions: sparse medium-sized sub-rounded quartz, moderate quantities of very fine mica, and sparse medium or coarse rounded brown grog fragments.

W2   White or pale pink surfaces and core. Hard rough fabric with a hackly fracture containing abundant medium or coarse quartz and moderate amounts of coarse rounded iron ore.

W3   Buff/yellow surfaces, pale pink core. Soft smooth fabric with fine fracture. Inclusions of moderate medium/fine angular quartzite, sparse very coarse rounded organic voids, and sparse very coarse red grog.

W4   White surfaces and core. Soft soapy fabric with fine fracture containing moderate to common sub-rounded quartzite, and sparse rounded red grog.

W5   Light buff surfaces and core. Hard rough fabric with fine fracture containing common fine quartz inclusions.

W6   Buff surfaces and core. Hard or very hard rough fabric containing common medium or coarse quartz grains and moderate amounts of rounded red grog.

The relative proportions of each fabric identified in each phase assemblage, and overall are shown in Figure 44 and Table 4.

Forms

As mentioned above, the site form series prepared during analysis will not be presented in this report. The range of forms present in each phase is illustrated below (Figures 36–42 for Site 1555; Figure 43 for Site 1515). Considering the assemblage as a whole it can be seen that a domestic range of vessel types is present, with jars, bowls, dishes and beakers, flagons, storage vessels, mortaria and strainers represented.

Jars are the most common form distinguished (189 possible separate vessels, 439 sherds), with examples recorded in all the main fabrics. Sherds of possibly thirty-one jars appear to have become sooted externally, or to have become encrusted with thicker carbonised deposits as a result of having been used for cooking over fires. This sooting was restricted to the reduced ware fabrics, particularly the gritty local R4, and to one coarse oxidised OX2 vessel; this phenomenon agrees with commonsense and the recorded evidence on other sites, where vessels using the coarser fabric types were used for cooking and the finer wares kept for other purposes.

The small number of larger storage vessels recorded again make use of the coarser fabrics, with R4 accounting for 49% of the total. A range of other reduced, grey and oxidised fabric types are also present. The forms

Fabric	Phase 1	Phase 2	Phase 3	Phase 4	Phase 5	Unphased	TOTAL	%
G1	14	604	271			245	1140	*2.05*
G2	19	1848	1305	301	6	2159	8090	*14.53*
G3	0	97		4	2458		101	*0.18*
G4	0	738	590	6	174	174	1682	*3.02*
G5	98	1022	1436	204	1176	2021	5957	*10.70*
G6	0	1	38		17	4	60	*0.11*
G7	0	8	78		131	26	243	*0.44*
NVCC					513		513	*0.92*
OX1	36	614	279	19	92	208	1248	*2.24*
OX2	12	275	1253	12	52	107	1711	*3.07*
OX3	28	523	1290	100	759	428	3128	*5.62*
OX4	6	248	192	2	7	158	613	*1.10*
OX5	3	87	381	3	38	139	651	*1.17*
OX6	41	113	98	5	21	65	343	*0.62*
OX7		60	13			35	108	*0.19*
OX8		1				247	248	*0.45*
OX9	116	519	9		57	18	719	*1.29*
OX10		43			62	76	181	*0.33*
OX11			19			28	47	*0.08*
R1	13	845	561	15	177	927	2538	*4.56*
R2	200	2548	2008	304	555	1076	6691	*12.02*
R3		243	673	12		91	1019	*1.83*
R4	1388	3967	1655	247	1318	6055	14630	*26.27*
R5		208	23		14	37	463	*0.83*
R6		298	94	10	132	147	500	*0.90*
R7	4	57	211	8	224	35	539	*0.97*
W1		38	37	3			78	*0.14*
W2		156	268	35		61	520	*0.93*
W3	2	43		13		96	154	*0.28*
W4		57	40	13	6	13	129	*0.23*
W5	3	76	405	66	393	296	1239	*2.23*
W6	25			128	138	16	307	*0.55*
Med						17	17	*0.03*
Grimston						55	55	*0.10*
PM		19					19	*0.03*
TOTAL	2008	15356	13227	1510	8520	15060	55681	*100*

Table 4 Coarse pottery fabrics, summary of sherd mass for all phases

represented are similar to the other jars in shape, but larger and thickened.

The number of bowls represented was smaller, with 54 possible individual bowls (74 sherds) identified. The sherds were distributed between sixteen different fabrics, but the main types present were rough handmade vessels in R4, common on the earlier phases, and wheel-thrown examples in the main grey fabrics G2 and G5 in later contexts. Fragments of an R4 bowl with a pierced base were found in a Phase 3 ditch (Figure 39 No. 41); this forms the only possible strainer found on the site.

Flagons were recorded in eight separate fabrics, with 126 sherds from up to 40 vessels identified, although two of these fabrics (OX11 and R2) are represented as single sherds. The remaining fabrics include all five white ware types, and the two main oxidised types (OX3, OX4).

Beakers and other drinking forms were identified in nine fabrics, comprising 93 sherds from a maximum of 17 vessels. Nene Valley colour coated wares were numerically the most significant type, with the remainder spread between the three main grey wares (G2, G4, G5), OX3, OX4 and the reduced wares R2 and R6. Numerically the most significant fabric is R2 (52%), but this is due to a complete, fragmentary beaker found in Grave *549* (Figure 41 No. 52). Folded beakers were found in the Nene Valley fabrics, but also in OX4, G2 and G4.

Dishes are a minor element in the form repertoire, and only five sherds were identified, one each in R2, R4, G5, OX1, OX6.

Residuality and Redeposition

A broad assessment of the degree to which the pottery recovered during the 1989 excavations on Site 1555 was found in its primary location or as secondary deposition should be attempted, as this will affect the conclusions that can be drawn from the evidence, both in terms of dating and for the functional variations suggested across the site.

It is apparent that some of the ceramic assemblage was transported some distance from its place of breakage to be buried on the excavation site. This process has been demonstrated most clearly with the fragments of brick and tile recovered, as there is no evidence for this material being used on Site 1555 and the entire assemblage should be considered as rubbish in secondary locations.

If the principle of rubbish transport is accepted, its extent must also be gauged. Unfortunately, obviously-

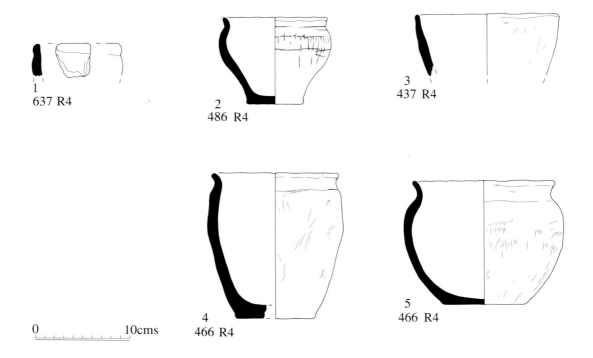

1
637 R4

2
486 R4

3
437 R4

4
466 R4

5
466 R4

0 _____ 10cms

Figure 36 Phase 1 pottery assemblage. Scale 1:4

introduced material such as brick and tile is not widely found across the site and appears to be restricted to the latest features (such as the fill of Well 1). Another index which may indicate a redeposition of material is the amount of residual pottery present. This may reflect the possible transport of pottery from its original location (though other causes must not be ruled out).

Using this aspect of the ceramic assemblage, the presence of 'early' R4 sherds in the latest backfill of Well 1 provides further evidence for the presence of transported/disturbed material in this deposit. Other deposits which appear to have a particularly strong residual element are the fills of pit *386* and ditches *495* and *514* in Phase 3; and pit *713* in the final Phase 5. This should not be taken as a gospel list of features containing at least some residual material, but does demonstrate that this is a factor to be considered in dating and interpreting the site.

Phase Ceramic Summaries

Phase 1 *(mid first century AD)*
(Figure 36)
In this early phase the predominant fabric represented is the reduced local gritty ware, R4, accounting for 1388g of the phase total of 2008g. The huge number of crucible fragments in fabric R6 recovered from the industrial pit *730* have not been included in this description as they relate more to industrial activities on the site than the domestic aspect evident in the other pottery.

Fabric R4 is present mainly in the form of handmade burnished vessels, though the examples from the flat-bottomed ditch *381* at 530mN were wheel-thrown. Recognisable forms were rare, but appeared similar to late Iron Age types recorded on other sites (*e.g.* Fison Way, Thetford (Gregory 1991)). The curvature and the external sooting of some body sherds suggests a range of cooking

jars or bowls; one bowl was recovered from the vicinity of the Phase 1 House.

Romanised forms and the characteristic grey fabrics of later phases are almost completely absent. A total of four sherds (117g) of the main grey wares, G2 and G5, were found in contexts associated with House 1, of these two were from an abnormal G5 handmade jar with poorly-fired surfaces; two further jar sherds were recovered from the waste pit *730*.

The distribution of the pottery across the site in this earliest phase is heavily biased towards the central area, in the vicinity of House 1, with only a single OX3 jar rim being recorded further north, and single body sherds of OX3, R2 and R4 coming from the industrial waste pit.

Illustrated Pottery
(Figure 36)
A full phase catalogue is included in the archive report (Section 6) and only a summary catalogue illustrating the diagnostic forms is included here. The catalogue text identifies the fabric, context, and working drawing/site form series number for each vessel, and describes any variations from the basic fabric definition.

1. R4 Handmade. *(637, Fill of House 1 ring ditch 388) 328.1*
2. R4 Handmade. *(486, Fill of pit 520) 420.1*
3. R4 Handmade. *(437, Fill of House 1 ring ditch 388) 441.1*
4. R4 Handmade. *(466, Fill of ditch 465) 473.1*
5. R4 Handmade. *(466, Fill of ditch 465) 447.2*

Phase 2 *(late first/ early second century AD)*
(Figures 37, 38)
Ceramic finds allocated to this phase comprise a greater quantity and variety of coarse pottery than is present in Phase 1, larger samian assemblages, mortaria, and significant quantities of fired clay objects and artefacts.

The coarse pottery phase assemblage consists mainly of the gritty local reduced pottery, R4 (as it did in contexts allocated to Phase 1), but some 'romanised' grey wares begin to make their presence felt. The grey ware

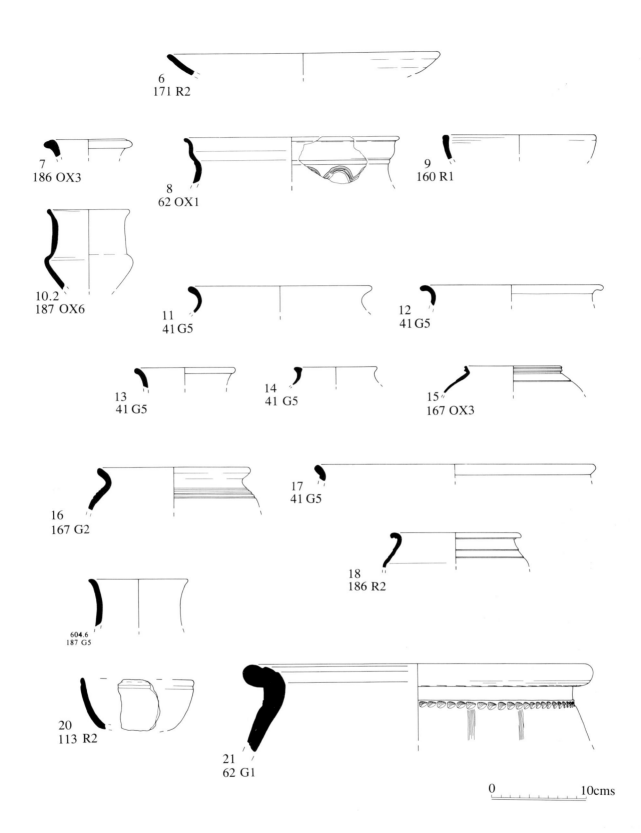

6
171 R2

7
186 OX3

8
62 OX1

9
160 R1

10.2
187 OX6

11
41 G5

12
41 G5

13
41 G5

14
41 G5

15
167 OX3

16
167 G2

17
41 G5

18
186 R2

604.6
187 G5

20
113 R2

21
62 G1

0   10cms

Figure 37 House 2 pottery assemblage. Scale 1:4

proportion of the overall assemblage is small in this phase, and includes some handmade forms absent in later phases.

The ceramic assemblage from the area of House 2 (*i.e.* between 730mN and 760mN) is rather different, and would appear stylistically to have a slightly later date. This may be reflection of the uncertainties expressed about allocating features to phases across the site and the problem of residuality, but may be an expression of functional differences evident in the waste disposal patterns around buildings and in other ditches.

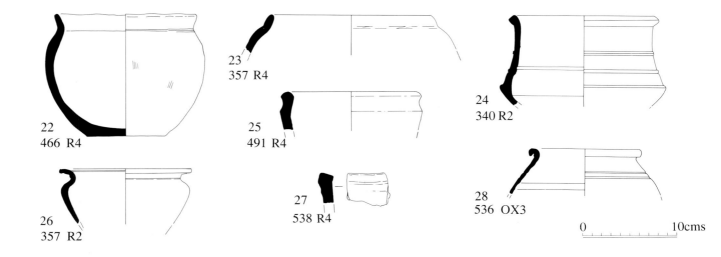

Figure 38 Phase 2 pottery assemblage. Scale 1:4

Illustrated Pottery
(Figures 37, 38)

House 2 and Enclosure
6.   R2 *(171, Fill of ring ditch segment 39). 101.1*
7.   OX3 *(186 , Enclosure ditch fill). 301.1*
8.   OX1 *(62, Fill of ring ditch segment 39). 306.1*
9.   R1 *(160, Enclosure ditch fill). 308.0*
10. OX6 *(187, Enclosure ditch fill). 310.0*
11. G5 *(41, Enclosure ditch fill). 403.1*
12. G5 *(41, Enclosure ditch fill). 404.1*
13. G5 *(41, Enclosure ditch fill). 405.1*
14. G5 *(41, Enclosure ditch fill). 410.2*
15. OX3 *(167, Fill of ring ditch segment 166). 412.2*
16. G2 *(167, Fill of ring ditch segment 166). 413.2*
17. G5 *(41, Enclosure ditch fill). 411.1*
18. R2 *(186, Enclosure ditch fill). 414.2*
19. G5 *(187, Enclosure ditch fill). 604.6*
20. R2 *(113, Fill of ring ditch segment 111). 309.10*
21. G1 Storage Jar *(62, Fill of ring ditch segment 39). 901.0*

Other Phase Assemblage
22. R4 Handmade. *(466, Fill of ditch 465). 447.0*
23. R4 *(357, Fill of gully 420) 419.2*
24. R4 *(340, Fill of ditch 352) 418.0*
25. R4 *(491, Fill of ditch 490) 421.1*
26. R2 *(357, Fill of gully 420) 303.1*
27. R4 Handmade. *(358, Fill of hollow) 431.0*
28. OX3 *(536, Fill of pit 559) 430.2*

Phase 3 (early–mid second century AD)
(Figures 39–40)
The assemblage shows a wider diversity of fabrics than in previous phases. The 'early' fabrics such as the gritty R4, are still present (particularly as residual material in the central part of the site) but are found in roughly comparable quantities to the romanised grey wares G2 and G5 typical of the later phases of the site. The single samian fragment from contexts assigned to this phase appears to be rather earlier in date than the phasing would imply, being conventionally datable to the period before AD70–85; however it is reasonable to assume that the sherd may be residual, given the larger quantities of datable coarse pottery recovered.

Illustrated Pottery
(Figure 39)
29. G2 *(246, Fill of pit 260). 415.2*
30. G2 *(531, Fill of ditch 589). 422.1*
31. G2 *(242, Fill of northern trackway ditch 245) 502.1*
32. G2 *(356, Fill of pit 386). 302.1*
33. R2 *(531, Fill of ditch 589). 424.1*
34. G5 *(531, Fill of ditch 589). 426.1*
35. R2 *(246, Fill of pit 260). 416.2*
36. R1 *(284, Fill of trackway ditch 245). 417.2*
37. R3 *(330, Fill of trackway ditch 285). 311.2*
38. R3 *(531, Fill of ditch 589). 423.1*
39. OX1 *(531, Fill of ditch 589). 429.1*
40. OX4 Decorated with panels of light combed decoration. *(242, Fill of trackway ditch 245)*
41. R4 Joining sherds in cleaning layers. *(576, Fill of southern trackway ditch 575). 801.1*
42. OX4 *(242, Fill of northern trackway ditch 245) 446.1*
43. R4 *(284, Fill of trackway ditch 245). 409.1*
44. OX4 *(296, Fill of trackway ditch 245). 601.1*

(Figure 40)
45. OX2 *(261, Fill of trackway ditch 245). 904.0*
46. G2 *(246, Fill of pit 260). 406.1*
47. OX5 *(246, Fill of pit 260). 407.1*
48. OX2 *(261, Fill of ditch 242). 905.0*
49. OX4 Handmade *(242, Fill of trackway ditch 245). 446.1*
50   R4 *(512, Fill of ditch 514). 425.04*

Phase 4 (late second century AD)
(Figure 41)
The most common fabrics were the hard grey ware G2 (36% by mass) and the two main reduced fabrics, R2 and R4, though fabric G5 was also present as a significant minor element. The range of forms present comprised sherds from five bowls, two flagons, and five jars, and the virtually complete R2 globular beaker from the inhumation burial *534*. Analysis of the distribution of these forms across the site shows a marked difference: four of the five jars recorded came from the small trackway ditch assemblage, while all the flagon sherds and four of the five bowls were discarded in the area of Enclosure 7.

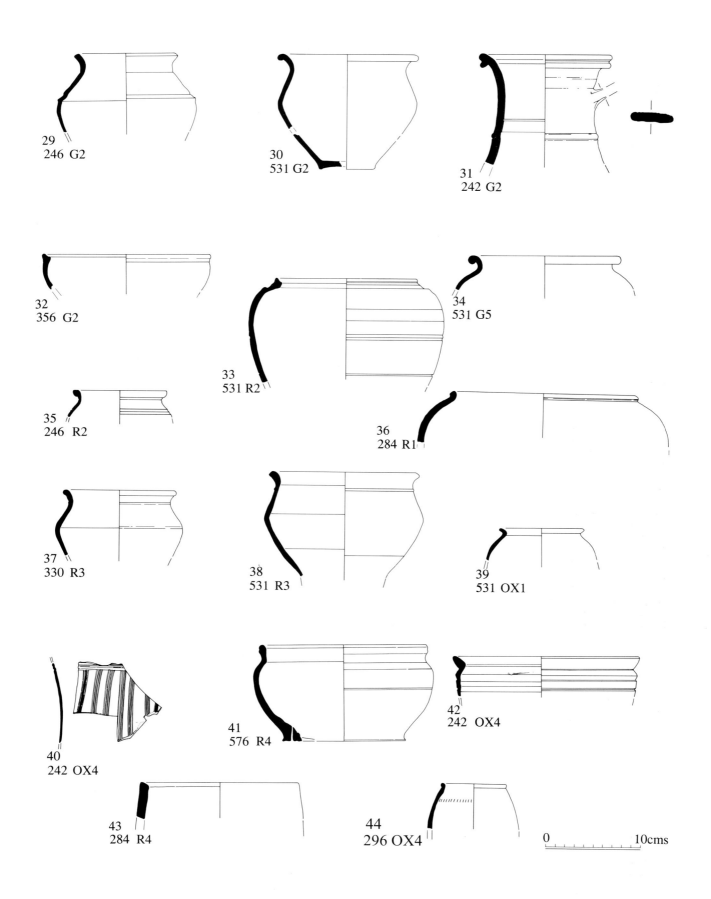

29
246 G2

30
531 G2

31
242 G2

32
356 G2

33
531 R2

34
531 G5

35
246 R2

36
284 R1

37
330 R3

38
531 R3

39
531 OX1

40
242 OX4

41
576 R4

42
242 OX4

43
284 R4

44
296 OX4

0   10cms

Figure 39 Phase 3 pottery assemblage. Scale 1:4

Illustrated Pottery
(Figure 41)
51. W5 (632, Construction backfill of Well 2). 321.1
52. R2 Shattered but complete beaker positioned adjacent to head, to right of inhumation. SF65. (534, Fill of grave 549). 606.0
53. G2 Black burnished surface. (564, Backfill of Well 2). 313.2.

Phase 5 (third century AD)
(Figure 42)
This phase represents the last activity on the excavated site and accounts for a small proportion of the total ceramic assemblage. The only securely stratified feature producing appreciable quantities of material was Well 1, where the final in-filling of the well shaft has been assigned to Phase 5. This naturally included a substantial amount of residual material but also contained diagnostic late forms and fabrics.

Well 1 Illustrated Assemblage
(Figure 42)
54. G1 (690, Lowest infill layer) 443.2
55. NV Folded Beaker, painted scroll decoration. (657, Demolition layers) 605.5
56. R4 (680, Demolition layers) 316.1
57. G5 (634, Bulk backfilling layer) 320.1
58. G2 (657, Demolition layers) 607.1
59. W5 Exterior burnt. (657, Demolition layers) 317.1
60. G2 (634, Bulk backfilling layer) 466.2
61. R4 (680, Demolition layers) 467.2
62. W5 (678, Silting/infill layer) 504.2
63. G5 (634, Bulk backfilling layer) 469.2
64. OX4 (634, Bulk backfilling layer) 475.1
65. OX4 (634, Bulk backfilling layer) 470.1

Site 1515
The Watching Brief kept on road construction identified a further concentration of Romano-British material to the north of the 1989 excavation (Site 1555), immediately north of the river Ingol: SMR Site 1515. The features and a summary of the pottery recovered from this site has been presented above (Chapter 5).

Illustrated Pottery
(Figure 43)
66. G1 (Fill of trackway ditch 16) 1515.01
67. R3 (Fill of trackway ditch 16) 1515.02
68. G2 Waster. Surfaces distorted by large number of burst air bubbles. (Fill of trackway ditch 16) 1515.03
69. R2 Imperfect vessel. Sides slumped prior to firing. (Fill of trackway ditch 16) 1515.04
70. R2 (Fill of trackway ditch 16) 1515.05
71. G1 (Fill of trackway ditch 16) 1515.06
72. G5 (Fill of trackway ditch 16) 1515.07
73. OX6 (Fill of trackway ditch 16) 1515.08
74. G5 (Fill of trackway ditch 16) 1515.10
75. R2 (Fill of trackway ditch 16) 1515.11
76. R2 (Fill of trackway ditch 16) 1515.12
77. G4 (Fill of trackway ditch 16) 1515.13
78. G2 (Fill of trackway ditch 16) 1515.14
79. G4 (Fill of trackway ditch 16) 1515.15
80. R4 Rusticated jar. (21 Fill of trackway ditch 16) 1515.16
81. R2 (Fill of pit 22) 1515.17
82. R2 (31, Fill of ditch 33) 1515.18

Discussion

The pottery recovered from Site 1555 showed widespread occupation and use of this area in the early Roman period. On the basis of externally datable traded pottery types, such as samian and the Nene Valley wares, occupation appears to have started in the mid-late first century, with the earliest types being South Gaulish samian stylistically dated to the Flavian period. The earliest material recorded is very similar to stamped vessels dated *c*. 45–65AD, with

examples of different types being recovered from the Phase 1 industrial pit (*730*) and the Phase 2 dog burial (pit *40*); the latter must be residual, the former may be so.

Stratigraphically early features, such as House 1 in Phase 1, are characterised by ceramic assemblages dominated by the reduced gritty R4 (and its oxidised equivalent OX9), and the organic-tempered fabric OX2. Vessel forms include handmade bowls and storage jars with smoothed or burnished surfaces, or vertical combing. Stylistically these types look more to Iron Age traditions than Romano-British, and would appear to be restricted to the earliest stages of activity on the excavated site and to have been largely replaced by the end of the first century AD.

Grey wares and white wares are absent from the earliest features but become increasingly important in later deposits. The rise in the grey wares is mirrored by a decline in the 'early' wares, with the organic-tempered OX2 being restricted to the very earliest features. Of the grey wares, the hard grey G2 and the sandier G5 are the main fabrics present in all features, and remain the standard wares until the end of the site's occupation.

Deposits containing these Romano-British fabrics should be dated to the period between the end of the first century and the third, with closer possible dating being made on the proportion of the 'early' fabrics present. This dating method can only be approximate, as it takes no account of residuality or functional differences between deposits, but it does provide a rough standard by which to compare assemblages.

In the 'Late' features on the site, the presence of traded wares from the lower Nene Valley is diagnostic. Both grey wares and the colour-coated wares were present on the site, but never amounted to a major element in the assemblages. As the Nene Valley Grey Ware and colour-coated industries do not appear to have been established before the second quarter of the second century (Howe, Perrin and Mackreth 1980), deposits containing either of these wares would date to the mid–late second century, or later. The presence of folded beakers with painted decoration in the latest deposits would date these to the mid third century at the very earliest and probably to the latter part of that century.

The latest deposit (ceramically) on the site is the backfill of Well 1. The mortarium and Nene Valley wares from this deposit were typical of late third- or early fourth-century products, and this must be taken as an approximate date for the abandonment of the site. However, since this backfilling appears to have taken place after a period of disuse (see Murphy in Chapter 4) the site is likely to have been abandoned some years before this, and the lack of other real evidence for occupation after the early third century suggests that the area excavated was largely abandoned from the earlier part of that century.

The trading links revealed by the pottery assemblage show that from the early stages of occupation in this area reasonable access to traded products was available. The saturation coverage of native sites by early samian is shown here by the amounts of mid–late first-century types found on all parts of the excavation, and its continued use through until the apparent cessation of major occupation in the third century. The presence of small numbers of amphorae also can also be taken as an indication of the social network present.

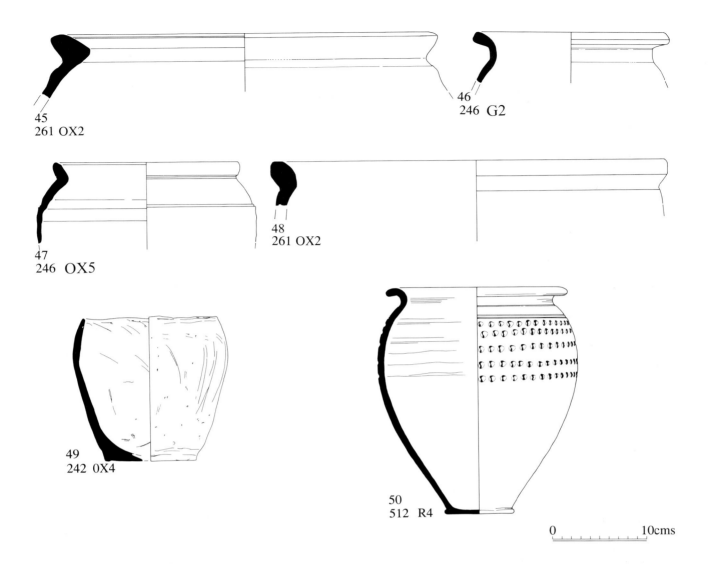

45
261 OX2

46
246 G2

47
246 OX5

48
261 OX2

49
242 0X4

50
512 R4

0   10cms

Figure 40 Phase 3 pottery assemblage. Scale 1:4

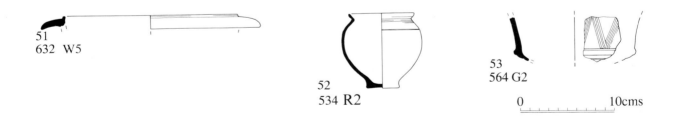

51
632 W5

52
534 R2

53
564 G2

0   10cms

Figure 41 Phase 4 pottery assemblage. Scale 1:4

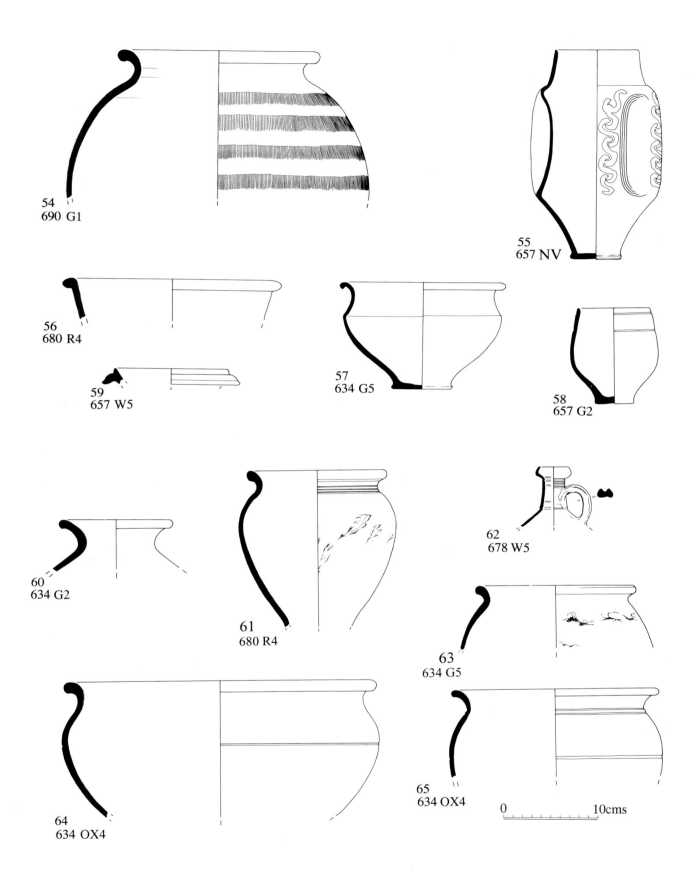

54
690 G1

55
657 NV

56
680 R4

59
657 W5

57
634 G5

58
657 G2

60
634 G2

61
680 R4

62
678 W5

63
634 G5

64
634 OX4

65
634 OX4

0   10cms

Figure 42 Pottery assemblage from Well 1. Scale 1:4

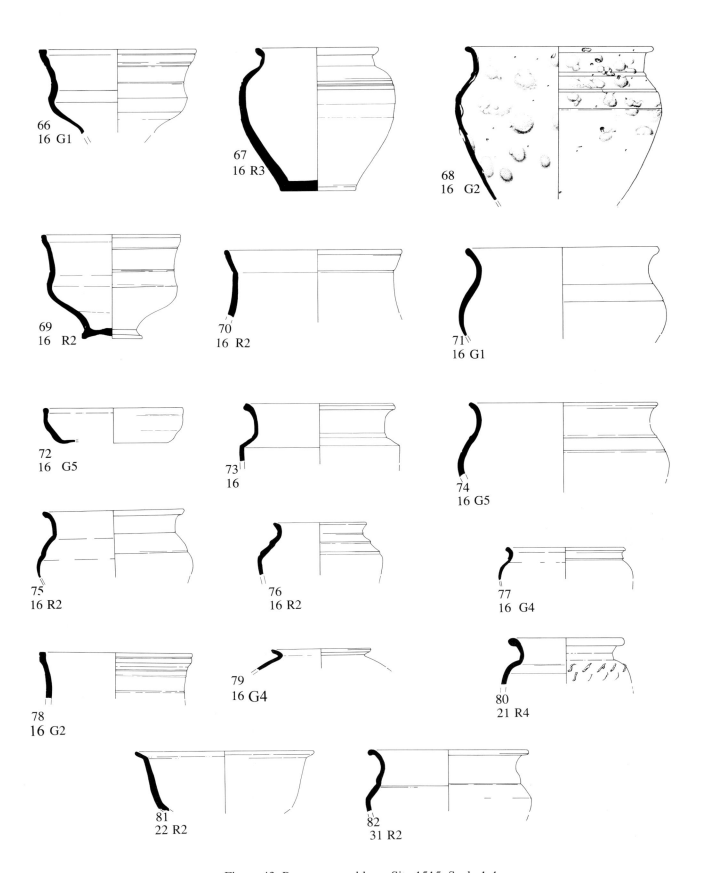

66
16 G1

67
16 R3

68
16 G2

69
16 R2

70
16 R2

71
16 G1

72
16 G5

73
16

74
16 G5

75
16 R2

76
16 R2

77
16 G4

78
16 G2

79
16 G4

80
21 R4

81
22 R2

82
31 R2

Figure 43 Pottery assemblage, Site 1515. Scale 1:4

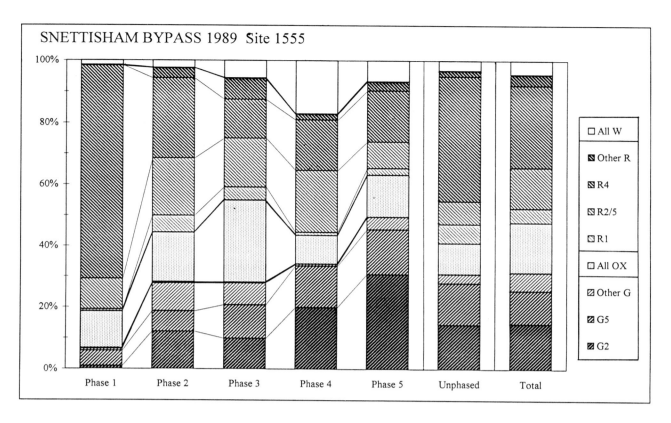

Figure 44 Pottery fabric proportions by phase, and total

However, it would appear that in general more localised trade was responsible for the pottery used on the site. The mortaria assemblage contains few recognisable products of the major industries, but appears to consist of local products from a number of (unknown) sources.

The coarse wares are again largely local wares, with the majority of the romanised fabrics (G1/R1, G2) apparently from kilns elsewhere in the Ingol valley (*e.g.* SMR Site 28450), a fact also supported by the waster sherds from the salvage excavation on Site 1515 (Chapter 5). What long-distance trade there was seems to have been restricted to the later phases of the site, from the mid second century on, when Nene Valley wares begin to be present. However, this never appears to a major element in the ceramic range used on the site. This is in rough accord with the later assemblage from the Saxon Shore fort at Brancaster (Andrews 1985) where local, Nar Valley, products were the major coarse ware, and Nene Valley products the main fine ware. The larger Nene Valley element in the assemblage at Brancaster can be explained by the chronological and social difference between the sites.

X. Brick and Tile
by M. Flitcroft
(Archive Report Section 4.10)

A total of 15.7kg of brick or tile was recovered during excavation at Site 1555 (288 fragments), including medieval and modern pieces as well as Romano-British material. There were no whole bricks or tiles, and very few large fragments. Twelve fabric-types were identified, of which five were post-medieval or modern, two medieval, and five probably Romano-British; the size of the

fragments made distinction between bricks and tiles impossible in many cases. Detailed fabric descriptions are included in the Archive Report (Section 4.10)

The distribution of the brick and tile over the site has few surprises. The medieval and later material was found solely in the ploughsoil, the Romano-British both in the ploughsoil and in stratified contexts. The small quantity of brick/tile recovered from the excavation, and the small percentage of large fragments within the assemblage, point to the absence of wide scale use of brick and tile on the site, a fact which is corroborated by the structural evidence. No structural evidence for Romano-British buildings either using brick or with tile inclusions was found on Site 1555 or during the Watching Brief and 1983 evaluation fieldwork.

Although most of the material recovered was medieval or later, sufficient numbers of Roman forms (*e.g. Tegula* or *Imbrex*) were found in stratified contexts to make it certain that material from 'romanised' buildings was being dumped on the site. No evidence for the reuse of these materials on the excavation site was found.

XI. Daub/Burnt Clay
by M. Flitcroft
(Archive Report Section 4.11)

The fired clay recovered from the excavation included loomweight fragments, pieces of daub and unidentifiable fragments of coarse ceramic. Where wattle impressions survive, they tend to be of young twigs and round wood with a diameter of around 15mm; a proportion have burnt-out plant marks on their surfaces. Two pieces retain thumb-prints where they were pressed into the wattle surface.

Loomweights

Thirty-two loomweight fragments were recorded, including four complete triangular weights, and eight sizeable fragments; all the recognised loomweights were triangular with pierced corners for suspension. The majority of recognised loomweight fragments were recovered from the vicinity of House 2 (in Phase 2) and they have been discussed as part of the site narrative at that point. The other fragments were recovered from ditch sections and from topsoil features across the site. No other concentrations of material were apparent.

The fabric of the loomweights is variable; most were manufactured in a coarse pale brown fabric, although pale pink and oxidised red-orange fabrics were also present. The complete weights all appeared to be equilateral triangles, but varied in size and weight from *c*. 800g to 1100g estimated original mass. All the identifiable weights are similar in shape and size to those from a broadly contemporary enclosure at Burgh, Suffolk described by Martin (1988).

The spatial patterning of the recognised loomweights outlined above (Chapter 4, Figure 15) in relation to the destruction of House 2, with a smaller concentration at the southern end of the associated enclosure ditch, is not paralleled around the earlier House 1, and no fired clay fragments which could (even speculatively) be identified as loomweights were found in this area.

There was a more general distribution of daub fragments than of loomweights across the site, but the concentration of material in the features associated with the removal of House 2 and the absence of similar finds around House 1 matches the pattern established for the loomweight fragments.

Chapter 7. Environmental Evidence

I. Human Bone
by S. Anderson
(Archive Report Section 5.1)

The human skeletal remains from this site consisted of a single inhumation and a redeposited child's jaw.

Inhumation 548: Grave 549
The inhumation (Plate VIII; also described in Chapter 4, Phase 4) was in extremely poor condition, being very friable, and most bones had been crushed by the weight of soil. Despite the fragmentary nature of the bone, all parts of the skeleton were represented to some extent.

Age and Sex
The skeleton is thought to be that of a man, based on the robusticity of the skull and long bones, and from the apparently narrow sciatic notch of the pelvis. Age was estimated from tooth wear at 45+ (Brothwell 1981); the general state of the skeleton also suggested an individual in old age.

Metrical and Non-metric Analyses
Very few measurements could be taken owing to the fragile nature of the bone. The palatal, meric and cnemic indices were the only ones which could be calculated. The limited results of both analyses are presented in the Archive Report (Section 5.1).

Dental Analysis
A table illustrating dentition state is included in the Archive Report (Section 5.1.5). Tooth wear was heavy, particularly on the maxillary teeth. Medium enamel hypoplasia, a condition thought to be related to childhood illness or malnutrition, was present on the incisors and canines. Medium calculus (tartar) was found on the lingual surface of the lower incisors, canines and premolars. There was slight alveolar resorption and a carious lesion on the right second maxillary molar. None of these traits are unusual for an individual living in the Roman period.

Pathology
Osteoarthritis was present on a number of articular surfaces, particularly in the neck area. New bone growth was detected in the left acetabulum and a number of muscle attachments, particularly on the femora and the tibiae. This growth can be associated with osteoarthritis or old age. Traces of periostitis (an infection of the outer layer of the bone) were noted in the leg bones.

Signs of physical trauma included traces of a compressed fracture of the skull; the degree of bone fusion along the fracture suggesting it occurred not long before death (possibly a matter of a few weeks or months).

A full description of the pathology is included in the Archive Report (Section 5.1.6).

Juvenile Mandible
This consisted of the left half of a juvenile mandible and one tooth from the right side of the mouth, and was recovered from the backfill of Well 1 where it must be considered as redeposited material. A table illustrating the dentition state is included in the Archive Report (Section 5.1.7). The estimated age from the state of eruption of the teeth is approximately 11–12 years; tooth wear on the permanent molars had reached the 2+ stage (Brothwell 1981). There was no calculus or enamel hypoplasia.

Discussion
The small amount of human remains is probably to be expected from the nature of the site. The reasons behind the interment of an old man just outside a settlement boundary rather than in a cemetery, and the deposition of a child's jaw in a well cannot be deduced from their mortal remains, and thus their importance in the interpretation of the site is limited. They do, however, provide some evidence of the physical aspects of daily life in a period contemporary with the use of the site (in the case of the articulated skeleton at least). It can be suggested that the possibility of surviving to old age was quite high, despite the evident physical hardship of life (shown in this case by the presence of arthritis and trauma, and the compressed fracture of the skull). Little more can be deduced on the basis of a single subject.

II. Animal Bone
by T. Ashwin
(Archive Report Section 5.2)

A relatively small quantity of animal bone was recovered during the 1989 excavations. Initial assessment by Rosemary Luff of the Cambridge Faunal Remains Unit suggested that the assemblage had little analytical potential and consequently it was decided to undertake a rapid identification scan.

Animal bone was retrieved from 161 contexts (21.2kg from 142 stratified contexts). Cattle bone was identified from seventy-nine contexts, sheep/goat from sixty-three, horse from twenty-six, pig from nineteen, dog from nine and red deer from two contexts. The dog remains included two entire skeletons. Bones of geese and ducks were also present in small numbers.

The largest concentrations of bone were from the vicinity of the Phase 1 House 1 and the ditches to the south of this structure, and from the backfill of Well 1, but elsewhere the quantities of bone from each context were often small. Due to the acid nature of the subsoil the bone was generally in poor condition and often heavily degraded. Butchery evidence, where noted, was usually represented by the chopping and splitting of cattle long bones.

III. Plant Macrofossils
by P. Murphy
(Archive Report Section 5.4)

Sampling at Site 1555 was on a small scale, and was confined to the investigation of the lower, waterlogged fills of the two wells, the fills of the 'corn-drier' *144* (Phase 3), and the fills of the round house ditches. Macrofossils preserved by waterlogging were recovered using the methods of Kenward *et al.* (1980). Carbonised remains were retrieved from fills of dry features by manual water flotation, using a 0.5mm collecting mesh.

Results

The Wells
A column sample was taken from Well 2 and individual context samples from the lower fills of Well 1. Plant macrofossil assemblages from all samples were characterised by abundant nutlets of *Urtica dioica* (nettle) with lesser amounts of other weeds, principally *Chenopodium album* (fat-hen), *Conium maculatum* (hemlock), *Rumex* spp (docks), and *Stellaria media*-type (chickweed). *Sambucus nigra* (elder) was consistently represented, and *Rubus fruticosus* (bramble) present. This is thought to indicate that local vegetation comprised a dense cover of nettles and tall perennial and biennial weeds, bramble and elder bushes and an annual weed flora in more disturbed areas. These well fills seem to relate to a period of abandonment when the immediate area became overgrown. Two fruits of *Triglochin maritima* (sea arrow grass) were noted from Well 2, which must have been derived from salt-marsh bordering the Wash. A few charred and uncharred cereal remains and a seed of *Papaver somniferum* (opium poppy) were present.

'Corn Drier' 144
Charred plant remains from two samples of flue deposits were examined. The sample from the upper deposit consisted largely of chaff (glume bases, rachis internodes, spikelet forks and awn fragments) of spelt (*Triticum spelta*), with traces of emmer (*Triticum dicoccum*), barley (*Hordeum* sp), wild or cultivated oats (*Avena* sp), a few wheat grains and small numbers of weed 'seeds'. The predominance of chaff implies that this sample was largely composed of a mixture of cereal by-products and wood, used as fuel. The second sample, from the fill of a previous flue, though including chaff and weed seeds, had a higher proportion of grains, mainly of wheat, most of which had germinated prior to charring. The predominance of sprouted wheat grain implies that this sample was a charred residue from malt-drying.

The Houses
Samples were taken at various points around the circumference of the ring ditches surrounding Houses 1 and 2. The samples included very sparse assemblages of charred cereal remains, weed seeds, hazel nutshell fragments and charcoal, with burnt and unburnt bone fragments. These may represent a low-density scatter of material derived from domestic hearths and other contexts, although slag fragments were also noted. Ericaceous charcoal was consistently present and some shoot fragments probably of *Calluna vulgaris* (ling) were noted, implying the use of fuels from nearby heathland.

The results of the analysis of samples from the house ring ditches, the wells, and the corn drier have been discussed above at the appropriate parts of the site description; tables indicating species present and relative proportions are included in the Archive Report (Section 5.4, Tables 1–4).

Conclusions
Archaeological evidence from the site indicates low-status domestic activity. The botanical results establish that malting, using spelt as the raw material, was another economic function of the site. Ample water supplies would have been required, hence the provision of at least two wells. The association of tentative or definite evidence for Roman malting with wells or low-lying locations close to streams is a recurrent pattern in eastern England. The macrofossils from the well-fills point to periodic abandonment of some areas of the site. No significant quantities of domestic food wastes (as opposed to crop processing waste) were present in the samples examined.

IV. Dendrochronology
by J. Hillam
(Archive Report Section 5.3)

The preserved timber linings of the two wells were sampled for tree-ring analysis with the aim of providing precise dates for the construction of the wells. All the samples were oak.

The timbers were of poor to moderate quality, especially compared to timbers used in some Saxon wells, such as those at Slough House Farm near Maldon in Essex (Hillam 1990) or Hamwic in Southampton (Hillam 1984a).

Results

Well 1
Four timbers from the well shaft lining, and two displaced planks recovered from the backfill were sampled. The well timbers were tangentially split from the outside of a single oak tree (the same ring pattern could be traced from sample to sample), and each contained 21–34 rings, giving a single sequence of 43 rings when combined in their matching positions. This sequence did not match the longer sequence from Well 2, or dated reference chronologies.

The two loose pieces were both planks shaped from very poor quality timber. Neither was suitable for dating (one had its ring sequence obscured by knots, the other had only 30 rings).

Well 2
Four timbers from the lining of Well 2 were sampled (Timbers *660,662,663,664*). These timbers were completely different to those from Well 1, being radially split oak. One timber *660* was very knotty and only the outer 63 rings could be measured; Timber *661* contained 65 wide rings. Timbers *663* and *664* contained 202 and 159 rings respectively. None had sapwood or bark.

The ring patterns of *663* and *664* were almost identical, suggesting that the timbers were split from the same tree. The tree must have been over 250 years old when felled, with a diameter of at least 0.7m. The tree from which *661* was felled may have been similar in size but, because it was fast grown, would have been much younger.

The ring widths of *663* and *664* were averaged to produce a master sequence of 202 years (detailed in Archive Report Section 5.3, Table 2). The master did not appear to match either of the other timbers from the structure. Comparison with dated reference chronologies for Droitwich, London, Mancetter and York (Groves and Hillam 1997; Tyers pers comm; Hillam 1984b; SDL unpublished respectively) suggested a statistically strong match for the date range spanning 112BC–AD90 (Archive Report Section 5.3, Table 3); this match was confirmed by visual comparison.

A precise felling date cannot be given because of the absence of sapwood. It is unlikely to have been felled before AD100 and, if no heartwood rings were lost when sapwood was removed, the tree would probably have been felled before AD145.

Further details of the samples are provided in the Archive Report (Section 5.3, Table 1)

Discussion

The results from the Well 2 timbers give a *terminus post quem* of AD100 for the construction of the well, and the 202-year chronology provides a new reference curve for the Roman period. It is a useful addition, even if it is probably based on only one tree, because Roman dendrochronology is dominated by chronologies from London and Carlisle. A more precise determination of the date of well construction cannot be given because of the absence of sapwood or bark from the samples, and the interval between tree felling and use of the timber.

No dating was obtained for the timbers from Well 1, nor is the 43-year ring sequence likely to date in the future. A ring sequence of 43 years is insufficiently unique for reliable dating.

Chapter 8. Discussion

I. The Local Setting: the 1989 excavations in relation to the Ingol valley

The area investigated in 1989 revealed only part of the original settlement in the Ingol valley, and this settlement was itself only a part of the pattern of land exploitation in this part of Norfolk. It is sensible to consider the evidence for this wider pattern and attempt to put the excavated area into some perspective.

The Ingol valley settlement is characterised by a network of rectilinear enclosures separated by ditched trackways. The enclosures are laid out approximately north-east/south-west to cover large portions of the south-facing valley floor. Within the complex small groups of circular structures have been noted on aerial photographs; these have many similarities with the round houses found during the 1989 excavations and suggest a general settlement pattern of dispersed activity centres set within extensive field or corral systems.

Despite the obvious importance of the area in the Iron Age, and the recovery of (unstratified) pre-Roman coins from Site 1555, the valley settlement does not appear to have been established until the mid-first century AD. Although the earliest features on Site 1555, such as House 1, included traditional 'Iron Age' pottery styles in their backfills, small quantities of romanised ceramics were also recovered, and should perhaps be seen as a forerunner of, or contemporary with, the widespread expansion into the Fenland environs of the early Roman period. The site continued to expand through the later first century into the second, and reached its greatest extent by the end of that century. After this the site seems to have experienced a gradual decline and apparent abandonment, although the final abandonment did not happen until the end of the third century, or even slightly later.

There is an apparent difference between the nature of the settlement north of the Site 1555 excavation (including SMR Sites 1515, 18236, 28450) where ditched tracks and roadways and relatively large enclosures are found and at least two possible hut circles can be seen, and the area south of the excavation (*e.g.* Sites 20199, 11829) where a series of rectangular field boundaries overlie each other. The northern part of this area seems to have been an industrial zone, with evidence for iron working, precious metallurgy and pottery manufacture, while the southern part appears to have been predominantly agricultural. Concentrations of domestic debris (pottery, tile) come from all parts of the settlement and while some of this can be interpreted as material carried out for dumping in field ditches, it would seem likely that the original occupation was similarly dispersed. Insufficient work has been carried out on the various surface assemblages from the valley to indicate whether these areas were all continually in use, or represent a less dense, shifting occupation but the settlement as a whole seems to have covered an area of around 100ha, putting it at the upper end of the scale established by Sylvia Hallam in her study of Fenland settlement in South-west Lincolnshire (Hallam 1970).

The economy of this whole zone appears to be of a widely mixed type. Agricultural production was the mainstay of the settlement, with spelt wheat production attested from the excavation area. However work on Fenland sites has suggested that this aspect of agriculture was, at best, secondary in this part of the country and that the main agricultural base was livestock rearing. Unfortunately the poor preservation of animal bone on both the excavation (Site 1555) and Site 1515 north of the Ingol makes identification of the relative proportions of species and their importance against other aspects of the site's economy unwise. The extensive systems of ditched trackways found on Site 1555 and visible in the surrounding cropmarks do imply widespread movement of stock between areas, and the construction of boundary ditches around both the houses similarly suggests the presence of animals requiring segregation. Sheep rearing can be suggested as forming part of this stock operation, with the animals providing wool for the weaving identified around the early second-century House 2, presumably also meat, and milk for cheese-making. By analogy with sites within the Fens, cattle raising may have also been a major part of the site economy, though the final product(s) (milk, skin, meat) cannot be recognised from the archaeological remains at Snettisham.

In addition to these agricultural aspects the valley settlement appears to have been involved in various forms of metallurgy. Unstratified iron smelting slag was recovered from the whole of the excavation area, and small fragments were recovered from many of the features, including the group of waste pits at the northern end of the site; three certain and several possible hearths were also found. This widespread distribution of smelting slag continued to the east of the excavation (including a hemispherical furnace base of 'Ashwicken' type) and to the south-west and also, to a lesser extent, to the north (Sites 1515 and 28450). Although slag was found all over the site the quantities recovered were light in comparison with true industrial iron-processing sites such as Ashwicken (Tylecote and Owles 1960) and it seems likely that this iron working only constituted a minor part of the settlement's economy, with production geared towards sufficiency rather than tradeable surplus.

Evidence for non-ferrous metallurgy is more limited, but still important. In the earliest phase of activity on Site 1555 copper alloy casting was being conducted, but appears to have been restricted to one location on the site. Silversmithing, in the form of jewellery manufacture, was apparently followed by at least one individual in the Ingol valley area, as the chance find of a second-century jewellery hoard at Strickland Avenue in 1985 indicates (SMR Site 1517; Potter 1986). Although both these more delicate forms of metalworking appear to have been definite sidelines in the site's economy, their presence may be an indicator of a continued metalworking tradition in this part of Norfolk.

From its foundation the settlement was a typical mixture of 'Roman' and 'native' in its character. The buildings on the site bore greater resemblance to Iron Age structures than Romano-British, but the social links were Roman with imported pottery and food occurring. The initial phase of occupation on the site shows some aspirations to Roman fashion in the use of grey ware pottery in wheel-thrown Romano-British forms, and the site's full acceptance of the new style can be seen from the second phase onwards as the local pottery industries began to produce 'romanised' wares. The site had access to the saturation imports of samian from the later first century onwards and this pottery seems to have found its way onto the site throughout its history; use of other imported products, such as Spanish olive oil and southern French wine can also be demonstrated. Links with other parts of the province of Britain were more limited. The brooches found on the excavation were typical of types current in East Anglia, though their actual source is unknown; much of the coarse pottery was obtained from largely unidentified local sources utilising fabrics similar to those used by the nebulous Nar Valley industry. The site could obtain the products of the Nene Valley potteries, based around *Durobrivae* (the modern Peterborough area) after this industry began to be widely traded in the later second century AD, and a few products from the Much Hadham kilns (in Hertfordshire) were recorded. The small number of coins lost on the site reflects both its largely early Roman date and the apparently general rarity of coinage on northern Fen-edge sites.

The architectural style appears to have been largely traditional, with single post-built circular houses being the norm. The fragments of roof tile found on the excavation and from surface collection in other parts of the valley indicate that some buildings in the settlement did aspire to Roman style, though these appear to have been a minority, and few real traces of such buildings have been found. Evidence from air photographs for the surrounding parts of the settlement suggests that there were few concentrations of buildings, with small groups of circular houses scattered around the square field enclosures.

II. The Regional Setting

The apparent third-century decline in the site (after Phase 3 on Site 1555) is a feature noted on many sites in the adjoining Fenland area (Hallam 1970; Potter 1981). This decline manifested itself most extremely in the southern, peat fen, zone where excavated sites show a temporary abandonment (for example, Welney (Phillips 1936, 1951)) associated with the deposition of large quantities of freshwater silt. This phenomenon is generally attributed to increased rainfall overloading the Fenland drainage system and leading to increased river bank erosion, the silting of channels, and consequent flooding. Further north on the silt fen and the surrounding skirtlands disruption appears to have been less severe as the land rose in elevation and was further removed from the choked river channels to the south. Many Fen-edge sites continued, in some form, through the third century and into the fourth (*e.g.* Denver and Leylands Farm, Hockwold (Gurney 1986)). The settlement at Snettisham falls into this second category; its elevation and location on the outer edge of the Fenland silts preserved it from the flooding experienced to the south, but the widespread changes of this period must have made the surrounding land on which it depended more marginal, and forced a reassessment of the viability of the area. It has also been shown (Waddelove and Waddelove 1990) that during the first four centuries AD the average sea level rose in southern and eastern England by several metres. This could also have had an incidental effect of reducing the viability of the site.

The apparent decline in activity on the valley floor is contrasted by the growth of settlement further east on the edge of the chalk escarpment, including the Park Farm Villa. This complex, overlooking the Ingol valley from the east, was partially excavated in the mid 1930s by H.C. Sheringham and produced third- to fourth-century pottery and evidence for a substantial romanised settlement. The dating of this site matches the period of decline in the excavated valley settlement, and it is possible that an increasing pressure on the low-lying land prompted a shift in emphasis to the higher land to the east which was well placed to exploit the uplands of the chalk. The continued activity on the valley site argues against a wholesale removal to the Park Farm area, but it is possible that the valley floor became an outlying part of an estate based further east.

The estate model put forward by Gregory (1982, 360–366) suggests that all the villas along the Icknield Way were located along the edge of the chalk escarpment in order to exploit the varied agricultural regimes of the high chalk lands, the river valleys discharging into the Wash, and the coastal plain. He notes an apparent absence of satellite settlements around any of the villas, and at Snettisham there even appears to be a decline in the existing valley floor settlement as the nearby villa flourished.

The Ingol valley settlement also has many morphological similarities with the (considerably more extensive) Fen-edge settlement at Hockwold-cum-Wilton (Salway 1970, Gurney 1986). Both settlements apparently consist of ditched trackways connecting series of large rectangular enclosures, within which were sited concentrations of buildings associated with evidence for industrial activities and livestock management. At Hockwold, as at Snettisham, the settlement expanded during the early second century AD before a decline in the later third century. Evidence for substantial (*e.g.* stone-founded) buildings on the Fen-edge site is better than at Snettisham, but the shift in the Snettisham settlement towards the Park Farm Villa and the presence of ceramic building materials both already discussed, does indicate the existence of some potentially similar buildings.

A final area of similarity to note is the religious activity in both areas. Whilst at Snettisham the pre-Roman Iron Age tradition is most spectacular (the Snettisham Treasure for instance) and at Hockwold the evidence is for later Roman buildings and deposits, both sites can be seen to have acted as religious or cultural foci (in addition to their other functions) and the ritual deposition of valuables in both areas are striking examples within a more widespread East Anglian phenomenon.

The Hockwold settlement has recently been included in a survey of Romano-British 'Small Towns' in Norfolk (Gurney 1995), but despite the obvious similarities between these two settlements a similar designation cannot be applied to the Ingol valley site without diluting an already vague term considerably further, and perhaps they should both be seen simply as examples of localised concentrations within the broader settlement pattern of this part of Norfolk.

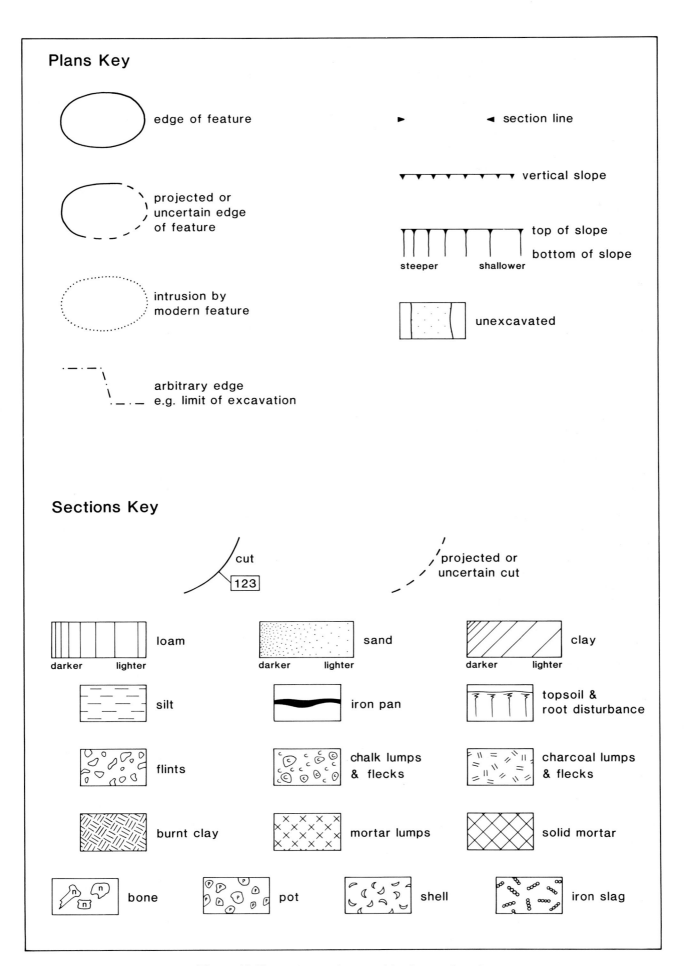

Figure 45 Key to conventions used in plans and sections

Appendix 1. Structure of the Archive Report

Introduction
This Appendix is intended to describe the contents and structure of the full archive report held by Norfolk Museums Service.

The published report is aimed at describing the nature of the site and the value of the results, rather than providing an exhaustive description of the project's findings. The full archive report provides the descriptive and interpretive information on which the published report is based. This includes description and discussion of all cultural features identified, quantification and analysis of all artefact classes, and statements of methodologies used throughout the excavation and post-excavation phases of the project.

The full archive report is organised in numbered sections to allow easier consultation and reference. It forms part of the larger project archive, which includes all the excavated material, and all the original site records (written, drawn, photographic). The archive report is cross-referenced to the original number sequences used during the excavation, and to the sequences used in the published report (where these differ).

Structure of Report
During the initial analysis of the site context information it was decided that the separate groups of features recorded during the excavation would form a suitable division of the site for descriptive purposes. Therefore nine groups were defined to cover the areas of archaeological remains.

GROUP 0 includes all features north of 760mN
GROUP 1 includes features between 725mN and 760mN
GROUP 2 includes features between 560mN and 600mN
GROUP 3 includes features between 515mN and 545mN
GROUP 4 includes features between 493mN and 506mN
GROUP 5 includes features between 460mN and 493mN
GROUP 6 includes features between 420mN and 460mN
GROUP 7 includes features between 360mN and 420mN
GROUP 8 includes features between 160mN and 210mN

Generally these groups relate to discrete areas of archaeological remains, with no direct stratigraphical link between individual groups. The exception to this is the relationship between Groups 4 and 5. These groups formed a single stratigraphical entity, but it was decided to split the area into two to separate the description of the house ring ditch in the northern part of the area from the later ditches to the south. The ring ditch and associated features were defined as Group 4, the ditches as Group 5. Each group was further subdivided into group phases on the basis of stratigraphy, alignment of features and artefact assemblage. These group phases were correlated across the groups to provide site phases. The allocation of identifying (or interpretative) numbers to the houses and enclosures on the site also followed this north-to-south sequence. A table mapping the (chronological) identifiers used in this published report onto the (geographical) identifiers in the Archive report is included at the start of Section 2 of the Archive Report.

The description of features and the analysis of the coarse pottery followed this division of the site, with the report broken down into discussions of each group with separate sections on each site phase represented.

Contents of the Archive Report
The archive report is ordered in the following sections:

1. Introduction, including topography, geology, methodologies
2. Description of features on site by group
3. Description of Watching Brief results
4. Specialist finds reports
5. Environmental/zoological reports
6. Coarse pottery report

Section 1. Archive Introduction
This section covers the same subjects as Chapters 2–4 of the published report, but separates the Watching Brief information from the excavation data (the former are part of Archive section 3 'The Watching Brief').

Section 2. Site Description and Discussion
This section describes all stratified contexts recorded during the main excavation. A table maps the publication structure numbers onto the Archive numbers. A standardised layout was adopted for this section to allow easier access to information.

The site is described from north to south according to the feature groups identified above (Groups 0–8).

Each group section adopts the same format. A copy of the relevant site plan, showing the features of the group is followed by a description of unphased features, followed by description and discussion of the features assigned to each phase. Major features, such as houses and wells, are described individually after the phase descriptions of their group.

Each phase description follows the same format.

1. A copy of the relevant site plan highlighting the features assigned to the phase.
2. Copies of site sections.
3. Transcript of site matrix.
4. Catalogue of contexts, ordered by cut and fill(s).
5. Description of features, discussing relationships.
6. Discussion of features.
7. Catalogue of bulk finds, ordered by cut and fill(s).

The individual descriptions of major features follow the same format as the phased features.

Section 3. Watching Brief Results
This section describes all the features recorded during topsoil removal over the whole bypass line, including the excavation area.

A series of maps record the location of the land units used in recording and describing the data. An Introduction outlines the scope of the Watching Brief and the methodologies employed.

A description of all features recorded during the Watching Brief follows, ordered from south to north by land division, with chainage from southern end. The two areas containing large numbers of contexts (excavation topsoil stripping and Site 1515 north of the Ingol) are described separately afterwards.

Firstly topsoil and Watching Brief contexts from the excavation area are considered, using an analogous format to the one used for stratified finds:

1. Catalogue of contexts
2. Description and discussion of contexts, ordered by group.
3. Catalogue of Bulk Finds

A description of features recorded in Site 1515, including location plan follows.

Section 4. Specialist Finds Reports

This section contains the full texts submitted by the specialists on the various classes of artefact from the excavation (Site 1555) and the other bypass sites.

Section 4.1 Iron Age Coins	T. Gregory
Section 4.2 Roman Coins	J. Davies
Section 4.3 Copper Alloy Brooches	D. Mackreth
Section 4.4 Slag Analysis	G. McDonnell
Section 4.5 Moulds and Crucibles	C. Mortimer
Section 4.6 Glass	J. Price and S. Cottam
Section 4.7 Samian	B. Dickinson
Section 4.8 Mortaria	D. Gurney
Section 4.9 Amphorae	D. Williams
Section 4.10 Brick and Tile	M. Flitcroft
Section 4.11 Fired Clay	M. Flitcroft
Section 4.12 Other Finds	M. Flitcroft
Stone Object	J.J. Wymer

Section 5. Environmental/Zoological Reports

This section contains the full text of the zoological, environmental and dendrochronological reports compiled for Site 1555.

Section 5.1 Human Skeletal Remains	S. Anderson
Section 5.2 Animal Bone	T. Ashwin
Section 5.3 Tree-ring Analysis	J. Hillam
Section 5.3 Plant Macrofossils	P. Murphy

Section 6. Coarse Pottery Report

This section comprises the results of the quantification and analysis of coarse pottery from Sites 1555 and 1515.

1. Introduction and methodology, Research Design.
2. Description of pottery assemblages, ordered by group and phase, followed by tabular summary of each group.
3. Discussion and comparison of assemblages from the houses, and from the wells.
4. General conclusions.
5. Catalogue of material, ordered by group and phase.

Bibliography

Andrews, G., 1985 — 'The Romano-British pottery from the 1974 and 1977 excavations' in Hinchliffe, J. and Sparey-Green, C., *Excavations at Brancaster, 1974 and 1977*, E. Anglian Archaeol. 23

Ashwin, T.M. and Whitmore, D. forthcoming — 'Excavation north of the river' in Ashwin, T.M., Gill, D. and Tester, A. (in prep), 'Excavations at Scole Romano-British Small Town, 1993–4'

Atkinson, D., 1914 — 'A Hoard of Samian Ware from Pompeii', *J. Roman Stud.* IV, 27–64

Bayley, J., 1990 — *Crucible Sherds from the Fishergate Excavation in York*, Ancient Monuments Laboratory Report 118/90

Boon, G.C., 1974 — 'Roman Glass from Caerwent, 1855–1925', *Monmouthshire Antiq.* 3 ii, 111–123

Brothwell, D., 1981 — *Digging Up Bones*, (Oxford University Press/ British Museum)

Casey, R. and Gallois, R.W., 1973 — 'The Sandringham Sands of Norfolk', *Proc. Yorkshire Geol. Soc.* 40(1), 1–22

Charlesworth, D., 1959 — 'Roman Glass in Northern Britain', *Archaeol. Aeliana* ser. 4, 37, 33–58

Charlesworth, D., 1966 — 'Roman Square Bottles', *J. Glass Stud.* 8, 26–40

Charlesworth, D., 1971 — 'A Group of Vessels from the Commandants House, Housesteads', *J. Glass Stud.* 13, 34–37

Clarke, R.R., 1952 — 'Notes on recent archaeological discoveries in Norfolk 1943–8', *Norfolk Archaeol.* 30, 156–9

Clarke, R.R., 1954 — 'The Early Iron Age Treasure from Snettisham, Norfolk', *Proc. Prehist. Soc.* 20(1), 27–86

Cunliffe, B., 1974 — *Iron Age Communities in Britain*, (Routledge and Kegan Paul, London)

Cunliffe, B., 1990 — 'Publishing in the City', *Antiquity* 64, 667—71

Darling, M.J. with Gurney, D.A., 1993 — *Caister-on-Sea Excavations by Charles Green, 1951–55*, E. Anglian Archaeol. 40

Dickinson, B. and Bird, J., 1985 — 'The samian ware' in Hinchliffe, J. with Green, C.S., *Excavations at Brancaster 1974 and 1977*, E. Anglian Archaeol. 23, 74–82

Dickinson, B. and Hartley, B.R., 1988 — 'Samian Pottery' in Martin, E., *Burgh: The Iron Age and Roman Enclosure*, E. Anglian Archaeol. 40, 30–34

Dickinson, B., 1993 — 'Samian Pottery' in Darling, M. with Gurney, D., *Caister-on-Sea Excavations by Charles Green 1951–55*, E. Anglian Archaeol. 60

English Heritage, 1991 — *Management of Archaeological Projects*, (Historic Buildings and Monuments Commission for England)

Erith, F.H. and Holbert, P.R., 1970 — Excavation at Vince's Farm, Ardleigh, Essex, *Colchester Archaeol. Group Bull.* 13(1)

Flitcroft, M., 1991 — *Archaeological Evaluation at Station Road, Snettisham*, (Norfolk Archaeological Unit Evaluation Report)

Gregory, T., 1982 — 'Romano-British Settlement in West Norfolk and on the Norfolk Fen Edge' in Miles, D. (ed.), *The Romano-British Countryside*, Brit. Archaeol. Rep. 103

Gregory, T., 1991 — *Excavations in Thetford 1980–82, Fison Way*, E. Anglian Archaeol. 53

Groves, C. and Hillam, J., 1997 — 'Tree-ring analysis and dating of timbers' in Hurst, J.D. (ed), *Multiperiod Saltmaking at Droitwich, Hereford and Worcester — excavations at Upwich 1983–4*, Counc. Brit. Archaeol. Res. Rep. 107, 121–6

Gurney, D.A., 1986 — *Settlement, Religion and Industry on the Fen-Edge; three Romano-British sites in Norfolk*, E. Anglian Archaeol. 31

Gurney, D.A., 1995 — 'Small Towns and Villages of Roman Norfolk. The evidence of surface and metal-detector finds' in Brown, A.E. (ed.), *Roman Small Towns in Eastern England and Beyond*, Oxbow Monogr. 52

Hallam, S.J., 1970 — 'Settlement around the Wash' in Phillips, C.W. (ed.), *The Fenland in Roman Times*, Royal Geographical Soc. Res. Ser. 5, 22–113, (London)

Harden, D.B., 1958 — 'Four Roman Glasses from Hauxton Mill, Cambridge, 1870' in Liversedge, J., 'Roman Discoveries from Hauxton', *Proc. Cambridge Antiq. Soc.* 61, Appendix 1, 12–16

Harden, D.B., 1962 — 'Glass in Roman York' in *An Inventory of the Historical Monuments in the City of York, I: Eburacum*, Roy. Comm. Hist. Mon., 136–141

Harden, D.B., 1977 — 'Roman Glass' in Rahtz, P.A. and Greenfield, E., 'Excavations at Chew Valley Lake, Somerset', *Dept. Environment Archaeol. Rep.* 8, 287–290

Hartley, B.R. and Dickinson, B.M., 1982 — 'The Samian' in Wacher, J. and McWhirr, A., *Cirencester Excavations I. Early Roman Occupation at Cirencester*, 119–46, (Cirencester)

Hartley, B.R. and Dickinson, B., 1990 — 'The samian' in West, S., *West Stow, Suffolk: The Prehistoric and Romano-British Occupation*, E. Anglian Archaeol. 48, 89–92

Hillam, J., 1984a — *Tree-ring analysis — Hamwic, Six Dials, 1981*, Ancient Monuments Laboratory Rep. 4167

Hillam, J., 1984b — *Tree-ring analysis — Mancetter excavation, 1977*, Ancient Monuments Laboratory Rep. 4169

Hillam, J., 1990 — *Tree-ring analysis of well timbers from Slough House Farm, Great Totham Parish, Essex*, Ancient Monuments Laboratory Rep. 81/90

Hinchliffe, J. and Sparey-Green, C., 1985 — *Excavations at Brancaster, 1974 and 1977*, E. Anglian Archaeol. 23

Howe, M.D., Perrin, J.R. and Mackreth, D.F., 1980 — *Roman Pottery from the Nene Galley: a guide*, (Peterborough)

Isings, C., 1957 — *Roman Glass from Dated Finds*, (Groningen)

Kenward, H.K, Hall, A.R. and Jones, A.K.G., 1980 — 'A tested set of techniques for the extraction of plant and animal macrofossils from waterlogged archaeological deposits', *Science and Archaeology* 22, 3–15

Knorr, R., 1909   'Ein Cannstatter Terra sigillata-Gefäss des Töpfers Sabinus und eine Rottweiler Schüssel des Sasmonos', *Fundberichte aus Schwaben* XVII, 26–30

Knorr, R., 1919   *Töpfer und Fabriken verzierter Terra-Sigillata des ersten Jahrhunderts*, (Stuttgart)

Laubenheimer, F., 1985   *La Production des Amphores en Narbonnaise*, (Paris)

Leah, M., 1994   *The Late Saxon and Medieval Pottery Industry of Grimston, Norfolk: Excavations 1962–92*, E. Anglian Archaeol. 64

Leah, M. and Flitcroft, M., 1993   'Field Survey at Park Farm, Snettisham and Courtyard Farm, Ringstead', *Norfolk Archaeol.* XLI, 462–481

Mackreth D.F., 1996   'The Brooches'in Jackson, R.P.J. and Potter, T.W., *Excavations at Stonea Cambridgeshire 1980–85,* (British Museum Press)

Martin, E., 1988   *Burgh: The Iron Age and Roman Enclosure*, E. Anglian Archaeol. 40

Martin-Kilcher, S., 1983   'Les amphores romaines a huile de Betique (Dressel 20 et 23) d'Augst (Colonia Augusta Rauricorum) et Kaiseraugst (Castrum Rauracense), Un rapport preliminaire' in Blazquez, J. and Remesal, J. (eds), *Produccion Y Comercio del Aceite en la Antiquidad* II, 337–347, Congresso, (Madrid)

Merrifield, R., 1987   *The Archaeology of Magic*, (London)

Millett, M., 1990   *The Romanisation of Britain*, Cambridge University Press, (Cambridge)

Peacock, D.P.S., 1978   'The Rhine and the problem of Gaulish wine in Britain' in du Plat Taylor, J. and Cleere, H. (eds), *Roman Shipping and Trade: Britain and the Roman Provinces*, Counc. Brit. Archaeol. Res. Rep. 24, 49–51

Peacock, D.P.S. and Williams, D.F., 1986   *Amphorae and the Roman Economy*, (London)

Phillips, C.W., 1936   'Roman Britain in 1935 in the Fens', *J. Roman Stud.* 26, 248–50

Phillips, C.W., 1951   'The Fenland Research Committee, its past achievements and future prospects', in Grimes, F.W. (ed.) *Aspects of Archaeology in Britain and Beyond*, (H.W. Edwards, London) 258–273

Potter, T., 1981   'The Roman Occupation of the Central Fenland, *Britannia* XII, 79–135

Potter, T., 1986   'A Roman Jeweller's Hoard from Snettisham, Norfolk, *Antiquity* 60, 137–139

Pryor, F., 1984   *Excavations at Fengate, Peterborough, England: the Fourth Report*, Northamptonshire Archaeol. Soc. Monogr. 2; Royal Ontario Museum Archaeology Monogr. 7

Salway, P., 1970   'The Roman Fenland' in Phillips, C.W. (ed.), *The Fenland in Roman Times*, Royal Geogr. Soc. (London)

Spratling, M.G., Tylecote, R.F., Kay, P.J., Jones, L., Wilson, C.M., Pettifer, K., Osborne, G., Craddock, P.T. and Biek, L., 1980   'An Iron Age Bronze Foundry at Gussage All Saints, Dorset: Preliminary Assessment of Technology' in Slater, E.A. and Tate, J.O., (eds), *Proceedings of the 16th Anternational Symposium on Archaeometry and Archaeological Prospection*, 268–292

Stead, I.M., 1991   'The Snettisham Treasure: Excavations in 1990', *Antiquity* 65, 447–465

Stead, I.M. and Rigby, V., 1989   *Verulamium: the King Harry Lane Site*, English Heritage Archaeol. Rep. 12

Tylecote, R.F. and Owles, E., 1960   'A second-century iron smelting site at Ashwicken, Norfolk', *Norfolk Archaeol.* XXXII, 142–163

Van der Veen, M., 1989   'Charred grain assemblages from Roman period corn driers in Britain', *Archaeol. J.* 146, 302–319

Waddelove, A.C. and Waddelove, E., 1990   'Archaeology and Research into Sea-Level during the Roman Era: Towards a methodology based on Highest Astronomical Tide', *Britannia* 21 253–266

Walker, D.R., 1988   'The Roman coins' in Cunliffe, B., *The Temple of Sulis Minerva at Bath — Volume 2, The Finds from the Sacred Spring*, Oxford Univ. Comm. Archaeol. Monogr. 16, 281–356

Williams, D.F. and Peacock, D.P.S., 1983   'The importation of olive-oil into Roman Britain' in Blazquez, J. and Remesal, J. (eds), *Produccion Y Comercio del Aceite en la Antiquidad* II, 263–280, Congresso, (Madrid)

Index

East Anglian Archaeology

is a serial publication sponsored by the Scole Archaeological Committee. Norfolk, Suffolk and Essex Archaeology Services, the Norwich Survey and the Fenland Project all contribute volumes to the series. It is the main vehicle for publishing final reports on archaeological excavations and surveys in the region. For information about titles in the series, visit **www.eaareports.org.uk**. Reports can be obtained from:

   Phil McMichael, Essex County Council Archaeology Section
   Fairfield Court, Fairfield Road, Braintree, Essex CM7 3YQ

or directly from the organisation publishing a particular volume.

Reports available so far:

No.1,   1975   Suffolk: various papers
No.2,   1976   Norfolk: various papers
No.3,   1977   Suffolk: various papers
No.4,   1976   Norfolk: Late Saxon town of Thetford
No.5,   1977   Norfolk: various papers on Roman sites
No.6,   1977   Norfolk: Spong Hill Anglo-Saxon cemetery, Part I
No.7,   1978   Norfolk: Bergh Apton Anglo-Saxon cemetery
No.8,   1978   Norfolk: various papers
No.9,   1980   Norfolk: North Elmham Park
No.10, 1980   Norfolk: village sites in Launditch Hundred
No.11, 1981   Norfolk: Spong Hill, Part II: Catalogue of Cremations
No.12, 1981   The barrows of East Anglia
No.13, 1981   Norwich: Eighteen centuries of pottery from Norwich
No.14, 1982   Norfolk: various papers
No.15, 1982   Norwich: Excavations in Norwich 1971–1978; Part I
No.16, 1982   Norfolk: Beaker domestic sites in the Fen-edge and East Anglia
No.17, 1983   Norfolk: Waterfront excavations and Thetford-type Ware production, Norwich
No.18, 1983   Norfolk: The archaeology of Witton
No.19, 1983   Norfolk: Two post-medieval earthenware pottery groups from Fulmodeston
No.20, 1983   Norfolk: Burgh Castle: excavation by Charles Green, 1958–61
No.21, 1984   Norfolk: Spong Hill, Part III: Catalogue of Inhumations
No.22, 1984   Norfolk: Excavations in Thetford, 1948–59 and 1973–80
No.23, 1985   Norfolk: Excavations at Brancaster 1974 and 1977
No.24, 1985   Suffolk: West Stow, the Anglo-Saxon village
No.25, 1985   Essex: Excavations by Mr H.P.Cooper on the Roman site at Hill Farm, Gestingthorpe, Essex
No.26, 1985   Norwich: Excavations in Norwich 1971–78; Part II
No.27, 1985   Cambridgeshire: The Fenland Project No.1: Archaeology and Environment in the Lower Welland valley
No.28, 1985   Norfolk: Excavations within the north-east bailey of Norwich Castle, 1978
No.29, 1986   Norfolk: Barrow excavations in Norfolk, 1950–82
No.30, 1986   Norfolk: Excavations at Thornham, Warham, Wighton and Caistor St. Edmund, Norfolk
No.31, 1986   Norfolk: Settlement, religion and industry on the Fen-edge; three Romano-British sites in Norfolk
No.32, 1987   Norfolk: Three Norman Churches in Norfolk
No.33, 1987   Essex: Excavation of a Cropmark Enclosure Complex at Woodham Walter, Essex, 1976 and An Assessment of Excavated Enclosures in Essex
No.34, 1987   Norfolk: Spong Hill, Part IV: Catalogue of Cremations
No.35, 1987   Cambridgeshire: The Fenland Project No.2: Fenland Landscapes and Settlement between Peterborough and March
No.36, 1987   Norfolk: The Anglo-Saxon Cemetery at Morningthorpe
No.37, 1987   Norfolk: Excavations at St Martin-at-Palace Plain, Norwich, 1981
No.38, 1987   Suffolk: The Anglo-Saxon Cemetery at Westgarth Gardens, Bury St Edmunds
No.39, 1988   Norfolk: Spong Hill, Part VI: Occupation during the 7th-2nd millennia BC
No.40, 1988   Suffolk: Burgh: The Iron Age and Roman Enclosure
No.41, 1988   Essex: Excavations at Great Dunmow, Essex: a Romano-British small town in the Trinovantian Civitas
No.42, 1988   Essex: Archaeology and Environment in South Essex, Rescue Archaeology along the Gray's By-pass 1979–80
No.43, 1988   Essex: Excavation at the North Ring, Mucking, Essex: A Late Bronze Age Enclosure
No.44, 1988   Norfolk: Six Deserted Villages in Norfolk
No.45, 1988   Norfolk: The Fenland Project No. 3: Marshland and the Nar Valley, Norfolk
No.46, 1989   Norfolk: The Deserted Medieval Village of Thuxton

No.47, 1989   Suffolk: West Stow, Suffolk: Early Anglo-Saxon Animal Husbandry
No.48, 1989   Suffolk: West Stow, Suffolk: The Prehistoric and Romano-British Occupations
No.49, 1990   Norfolk: The Evolution of Settlement in Three Parishes in South-East Norfolk
No.50, 1993   Proceedings of the Flatlands and Wetlands Conference
No.51, 1991   Norfolk: The Ruined and Disused Churches of Norfolk
No.52, 1991   Norfolk: The Fenland Project No. 4, The Wissey Embayment and Fen Causeway
No.53, 1992   Norfolk: Excavations in Thetford, 1980–82, Fison Way
No.54, 1992   Norfolk: The Iron Age Forts of Norfolk
No.55, 1992   Lincolnshire: The Fenland Project No.5: Lincolnshire Survey, The South-West Fens
No.56, 1992   Cambridgeshire: The Fenland Project No.6: The South-Western Cambridgeshire Fens
No.57, 1993   Norfolk and Lincolnshire: Excavations at Redgate Hill Hunstanton; and Tattershall Thorpe
No.58, 1993   Norwich: Households: The Medieval and Post-Medieval Finds from Norwich Survey Excavations 1971–1978
No.59, 1993   Fenland: The South-West Fen Dyke Survey Project 1982–86
No.60, 1993   Norfolk: Caister-on-Sea: Excavations by Charles Green, 1951–55
No.61, 1993   Fenland: The Fenland Project No.7: Excavations in Peterborough and the Lower Welland Valley 1960–1969
No.62, 1993   Norfolk: Excavations in Thetford by B.K. Davison, between 1964 and 1970
No.63, 1993   Norfolk: Illington: A Study of a Breckland Parish and its Anglo-Saxon Cemetery
No.64, 1994   Norfolk: The Late Saxon and Medieval Pottery Industry of Grimston: Excavations 1962–92
No.65, 1993   Suffolk: Settlements on Hill-tops: Seven Prehistoric Sites in Suffolk
No.66, 1993   Lincolnshire: The Fenland Project No.8: Lincolnshire Survey, the Northern Fen-Edge
No.67, 1994   Norfolk: Spong Hill, Part V: Catalogue of Cremations
No.68, 1994   Norfolk: Excavations at Fishergate, Norwich 1985
No.69, 1994   Norfolk: Spong Hill, Part VIII: The Cremations
No.70, 1994   Fenland: The Fenland Project No.9: Flandrian Environmental Change in Fenland
No.71, 1995   Essex: The Archaeology of the Essex Coast Vol.I: The Hullbridge Survey Project
No.72, 1995   Norfolk: Excavations at Redcastle Furze, Thetford, 1988–9
No.73, 1995   Norfolk: Spong Hill, Part VII: Iron Age, Roman and Early Saxon Settlement
No.74, 1995   Norfolk: A Late Neolithic, Saxon and Medieval Site at Middle Harling
No.75, 1995   Essex: North Shoebury: Settlement and Economy in South-east Essex 1500–AD1500
No.76, 1996   Nene Valley: Orton Hall Farm: A Roman and Early Anglo-Saxon Farmstead
No.77, 1996   Norfolk: Barrow Excavations in Norfolk, 1984–88
No.78, 1996   Norfolk:The Fenland Project No.11: The Wissey Embayment: Evidence for pre-Iron Age Occupation
No.79, 1996   Cambridgeshire: The Fenland Project No.10: Cambridgeshire Survey, the Isle of Ely and Wisbech
No.80, 1997   Norfolk: Barton Bendish and Caldecote: fieldwork in south-west Norfolk
No.81, 1997   Norfolk: Castle Rising Castle
No.82, 1998   Essex: Archaeology and the Landscape in the Lower Blackwater Valley
No.83, 1998   Essex: Excavations south of Chignall Roman Villa 1977–81
No.84, 1998   Suffolk: A Corpus of Anglo-Saxon Material
No.85, 1998   Suffolk: Towards a Landscape History of Walsham le Willows
No.86, 1998   Essex: Excavations at the Orsett 'Cock' Enclosure
No.87, 1999   Norfolk: Excavations in Thetford, North of the River, 1989–90
No.88, 1999   Essex: Excavations at Ivy Chimneys, Witham 1978–83
No.89, 1999   Lincolnshire: Salterns: Excavations at Helpringham, Holbeach St Johns and Bicker Haven
No.90, 1999   Essex:The Archaeology of Ardleigh, Excavations 1955–80
No.91, 2000   Norfolk: Excavations on the Norwich Southern Bypass, 1989–91 Part I Bixley, Caistor St Edmund, Trowse
No.92, 2000   Norfolk: Excavations on the Norwich Southern Bypass, 1989–91 Part II Harford Farm Anglo-Saxon Cemetery
No.93, 2001   Norfolk: Excavations on the Snettisham Bypass, 1989